D1001468

BARÇA

BLUME

Project editor Matt Lowing
Editorial Conor Kilgallon, Caroline Curtis and Steve Dobell
Picture Research Paul Langan and Steve Behan
Translation Marc Joss
Researcher Maribel Herruzo

© 2014 Art Blume, S. L.
Av. Mare de Déu de Lorda, 20
08034 Barcelona
Tel. 93 205 40 00 Fax 93 205 14 41
e-mail: info@blume.net
© 2014 Text and design layout FC Barcelona and Carlton Books Limited

ISBN: 978-84-9801-811-0

Printed in Slovenia

All rights reserved. No part of this book may be
reproduced in any printed or electronic form without
the permission of the publisher and the author.

WWW.BLUME.NET

BARÇA

The Illustrated History
of **FC Barcelona**

BLUME

Guillem Balagué

FCBARCELONA
OFFICIAL PRODUCT

CONTENTS

LEFT: The 2010–11 Barcelona team created history. They changed football when we all thought everything had been invented. It had the best player in the world, the best midfielders in the world, the ideal defenders, the best manager. The team finished the season with three trophies – *La Liga*, the Champions League and the *Supercopa de España*.

INTRODUCTION

The *Cant del Barça*, the official hymn of FC Barcelona, is performed before every home match. Commissioned in 1974 to celebrate the club's 75th anniversary, the hymn's music was composed by Manuel Valls and features lyrics by Jaume Picas and Josep Maria Espinàs. The words of *Cant del Barça* give an insight into why FC Barcelona is "més que un club" ("more than a club").

Tot el camp / és un clam
The whole stadium loudly cheers

[Industria, Les Corts and Camp Nou stadiums have all been the home to sporting triumphs, political declarations, cultural integration, emotional acts… and the place where some of the biggest stars in the history of football have been seen.]

Som la gent blaugrana
We're the Azulgrana people

[One possible version of the origin of the blue and red on the kit is that the colours were inspired by a pencil that happened to be on a table at Solé gymnasium, where the club was founded in 1899. Supporters have always known that this is a different club, which is why even a victory won't stop them from whistling and berating the team if they do not like the its style of play. They welcome big stars, but are terribly demanding – of the presidents, the star players, the coaches.]

Tant se val d'on venim / si del sud o del nord
It doesn't matter where we come from, be it the north or the south

[Founder Gamper was Swiss. Some of the first members, players and presidents were foreign. Throughout its history, Catalan supporters have always been joined by those who arrive in Catalonia seeking new opportunities. This is a club that integrates people, no matter what their culture or from where they come, and whose play and philosophy fascinate the masses.]

Ara, estem d'acord, estem d'acord / una bandera ens agermana
Now we all agree, we all agree, one flag unites us in brotherhood

[Origin does not matter when part of the same ideal – a common history and colours that are recognized the world over. Barça's flag is not only football, it represents important values.]

Blaugrana al vent / un crit valent
Azulgrana colours blowing in the wind, one valiant cry

[Especially during the hard times: wars, dictatorships, repression and unfair convictions, losses, defeats … at a club which, let us not forget, has always belonged to its members.]

**Tenim un nom, el sap tothom /
¡Barça, Barça, Baaaarça!**
***We have a name that everyone knows:
Barça, Barça, Baaaarça!***

[The origin of the shortened form Barça is unknown. It was first written down on November 30, 1922 in a weekly magazine called *Xut!*, and they say that the chant was used to encourage the team at the Les Corts ground. The word was banned in the media under Franco's regime, but made a return in 1955 thanks to the rise to prominence of a Catalan magazine that went by the same name. In the 1960s and 70s the word spread and nowadays identifies FC Barcelona the world over.]

LEFT: Few players represent the success, style and integrity of FC Barcelona as well as Lionel Messi does. The Argentine striker has been a key factor in the club's unparalleled success in recent years.

ABOVE: It is impossible not to be impressed by Barcelona's Camp Nou. Not to feel something special is about to happen. It is a place of pilgrimage for so many people all over the world...

Jugadors, seguidors / tots units fem força
Players, supporters, united we are strong

[This was the motto printed on the reverse of the crest for the 2010–11 shirt. Players have included: Luis Suárez, Ramallets, Samitier, Zamora, Basora, César Rodríguez, Kocsis, Kubala, Moreno and Manchón, Sadurní; Rexach, Cruyff, Neeskens, el Cholo Sotil, Asensi; Maradona, Schuster, Lineker, Koeman, Laudrup and Guardiola; Migueli, Alexanko, Zubizarreta, Amor, Begiristain, Simonsen, Quini; Stoichkov, Romário, Rivaldo and Ronaldo; Luis Enrique, Bakero, Lobo Carrasco; Ronaldinho, Deco, Eto'o, Rafa Márquez; Abidal, Alves. There have been eight World Cup winners: Valdés, Villa, Puyol, Xavi, Iniesta, Piqué, Pedro, Fábregas, Busquets. And, of course, Messi. Some of these players were home grown, others have arrived from other clubs, countries and continents – much like their supporters. The members of Fan Club Barça Polska, for example, created a banner 2,000m² printed with the slogan and the faces of Guardiola, Messi, Puyol and Cruyff.]

Som molts anys plens d'afanys
Many years of hard work

[To grow, to become and to remain among the best top clubs in the world, to find a unique style, to demonstrate singularity, to construct a new model, to create something as essential as the much-admired football school *La Masía*. Furthermore, Barça have always tried to be both local and universal, political and apolitical, to demonstrate *seny i rauxa* (*seny* – a form of ancestral Catalan wisdom or sensibleness; *rauxa* – sudden determination or action).]

Són molts gols que hem cridat
Many goals we have cheered

[Exciting, at the death, spectacular, unrepeatable,
celebrated, impossible, glory-clinching goals.
Goals by César and Kubala, Paulino Alcántara,
Evaristo's diving header, Ronaldo against
Compostela, goals from Cruyff, Romário,
Ronaldinho, the goal Puyol prevented with his
chest; 5–0 and 6–2 at the Bernabéu; Bakero
against Kaiserslautern, Koeman at Wembley,
Eto'o and Belletti in Paris, Eto'o and Messi in
Rome, Iniesta against Chelsea, Pedro,
Messi and Villa at Wembley once again, Messi
against Getafe and his four against Arsenal…]

I s'ha demostrat / que mai ningú no
ens podrà tòrcer
And we have shown that no one
can ever break us

[Not adversaries, nor impositions, nor furious
criticism, nor attacks, nor misunderstandings,
nor strange episodes behind the scenes.
Barça have been on the receiving end of attacks
by politicians, governments, the media, rival
teams, coaches – and proudly remain standing,
among the best in the world.]

Azulgrana blowing in the wind, one valiant cry,
the name of a club known the world over:
Barça, Barça, Baaaarça.

This is its story.

1. THE BIRTH OF A LEGENDARY CLUB

FC Barcelona was created by a group of young men who were united by nothing more than their love for a sport that was still unknown in Spain. This group was made up of just 12 members eager to run after a ball, and their captain, a 20-something Swiss, had only just moved to Barcelona to learn Spanish. He was Hans Gamper, a natural sportsman who, on October 22, 1899, travelled to the editorial office of the weekly publication *Los Deportes* to publish a brief eight-line note urging anyone who liked football to contact him "by kindly coming along to the office on Tuesday and Friday nights from 9 till 11". With this simple, polite invitation, Gamper and the 11 other enthusiasts founded FC Barcelona.

Their first meeting was on November 29, 1899 (the official date for the birth of the club) – and the venue for such an important moment? The Solé gymnasium. There were only just enough players for a match. Naturally enough, the name and badge were taken from the city of Barcelona. The club's colours – blue and red stripes – were chosen in the second meeting held on December 13. One odd theory is that the founders were inspired by the coloured pencils employed at the time in accountancy, which made use of colours from opposite ends of the spectrum. Whatever the real reason, the only aspects of Barça's kit to have changed over the years are the colour of the shorts (originally white), and the width of the stripes.

Gamper was joined on this adventure by his fellow Swiss countrymen Walter Wild and Otto Kunzle, Englishmen John and William Parsons, German Otto Maier, and Catalans Lluís d'Ossó, Bartomeu Terradas, Enric Ducal, Pere Cabot, Carles Pujol and Josep Llobet. Together, they formed a heterogeneous group in which nationality did not matter. Wild was the club's inaugural president, although only for five months.

He also played at the same time. Some of his fellow Barcelona members and players were Englishmen who played with Gamper on the pitch in the middle of the defunct Bonanova velodrome. This was the club's first venue, where they continued to play for months afterwards.

The first match in the club's history was played on December 8, 1899, although both teams managed to field only ten players. Barcelona daily newspaper *La Vanguardia* published a match report the following day in the sports section which read:

"Superb play yesterday in the ex-Bonanova velodrome, between 'Foot-ball Club de Barcelona' and some youngsters from the capital's English community. ... Team Barcelona started the match, and then followed that series of incidents which provide such attraction in this sport, a favourite in healthy nations. ... In the second half, the English team had Team Barcelona in check for a spell,

PREVIOUS PAGES:, Paulino Alcántara had two spells with FC Barcelona (1912–1916 and 1918–1927). A prolific goalscorer and fan favourite, he remains the youngest player to play or score for the club.

LEFT: Joan Gamper, the founder of FC Barcelona. He settled in the Catalan capital to learn Spanish, but it didn't take long for the inveterate sportsman and football lover to find some fellow fans with whom he could share his passion.

RIGHT: Walter Wild was one of the attendees at the founding meeting at the Solé gymnasium in 1899. As well as playing, he was the club's first president, a post which he held for 17 months.

RIGHT: The *Azulgranas* played their first match with just ten players on December 8, 1899, at the ex-Bonanova velodrome, as reported in the daily newspaper *La Vanguardia*.

BELOW: The first official competition in Spain, the *Copa Macaya* was FC Barcelona's first title in 1902. The tournament became the Catalan football championship one year later.

as they were camped in opposition territory for 15 minutes, until Barcelona captain Mr Gamper managed to drive towards the opponents' goal on one of his impulsive runs; he went for goal but to no avail. To finish, please allow us to warmly congratulate 'Foot-ball Club Barcelona' on commencing their sessions so promisingly and may we extend the congratulations to the youngsters from the English community (…). The party ended gaily, with the usual hip, hip, hoorays at such gatherings."

The recently founded Barcelona club lost their inaugural match by one goal, but just as the journalist wrote, the performance generated optimism and enthusiasm, which gained momentum over time. Barcelona did not move to another ground until November 18, 1900, almost a year after its formation. The new venue was the Hotel Casanovas, where they played and drew their first derby in December against Sociedad Española de Fútbol, which would later become Real Club Deportivo Español. One year after this, they relocated to Carretera de Horta, where they stayed until early 1905. The team then moved to play on a nameless pitch bordered by the Muntaner, Londres, París and Casanovas roads from February of that year until 1909.

Barcelona had already secured their first official title by then: the 1902 *Copa Macaya*, which would later be called the Catalan football championship. The Cup owed its name to the creator of the tournament, Alfons Macaya, president of the Hispania Atletic Club (a club formed mainly by resident Scottish workers in the Sant Andreu district of Barcelona), who

created what would be the first official footballing competition in Spain at the start of the twentieth century. Only Catalan clubs took part and the competition disappeared in 1940, when Franco's dictatorial regime prohibited any regional championships.

That first tournament victory was decisive because it enabled the club to secure the confidence of its members and fans by winning all eight matches played and scoring 60 goals, conceding only two. FC Barcelona would win the tournament the following year as well (by then known as the *Copa de Barcelona*) along with the Catalan championship in 1904–05 and 1908–09, the year of the inauguration of the Camp de la Indústria stadium. As well as achieving success in the *Copa Macaya*, the team finished runners-up against Vizcaya in the first *Campeonato de España* (today's *Copa del Rey*) in 1902. This was the tournament in which the club first faced the team that would become their eternal rivals – Real Madrid, known at the time as Madrid Club de Football. The fixture took place on May 13, 1902, only two months after the official formation of the Madrid club by two brothers, ironically also from Barcelona, Juan and Carlos Padrós. Barcelona took the honours in that inaugural *clásico* by three goals to one.

The 1903 season was Gamper's last as a player – he was 25 years old and wanted to devote more time to his business – although he did not abandon the club, which played its first international match that year in France against Stade Olympique, beating them by three goals to two. Football was gradually becoming popular

Los Deportes

Propagador de la Educación Física y cultura nacional
Apologista de los ejercicios corporales. Eco de las Sociedades de Sport
Revista semanal ilustrada, única en su clase en España

Año VII   Barcelona 31 Mayo de 1903   Núm. 22

Primer team del "Football Club Barcelona"
vencedor del concurso Copa del Club «Barcelona» (temporada 1902-903)

P. Cabot   F. Gass   V. Reig   J. Vidal

Ossó Steinberg Meyer Witty (cap.) Gamper Harris Lassaleta

LEFT: In May 1903 *Los Deportes*, the same magazine that had published Joan Gamper's advertisement, featured a squad photo on the front cover, which was a sign of the importance that football was acquiring in Spain.

and this was reflected in the press, as could be seen by the front cover of a May 1903 edition of *Los Deportes*, which featured Barcelona players posing for the camera.

From 1904 until the construction of the Camp de la Indústria stadium, both FC Barcelona and Espanyol (as they were now called) were becoming the powerhouses of Catalan football as the sport's popularity grew.

But sporting failures followed. The team managed to lose 10–1 against Bilbao in the 1905–06 season, and 9–1 against Olympique de Marseille in an unusually feisty match against a team made up of ex-rugby players. A fixture against a team known as simply as "X" and made up of many former Espanyol players, ended up with fists flying and the police had to intervene. Due to a lack of titles to offer the fans, FC Barcelona were losing members at an alarming rate to the point where at the start of the 1908 season they had only 38. The club was going through a deep crisis which took them to the brink of extinction. In fact, this affected Catalan football in general – Espanyol disappeared for three years. Hans Gamper, who now adopted the Catalan version of his name – Joan Gamper – had recently retired from business and until that point had been just a privileged observer of the club's affairs. He called a meeting that only around 20 people attended, where he decided to take over the reins at the club and get it back on track.

After officially taking over the presidency for the first time on December 2, 1908, Gamper decided to recover member numbers in a surprising way: by visiting them one by one and

convincing them to return. His effort paid off: by the following year the club had grown from 38 to 201. The founder's initiative was so decisive and his method so effective that some months later, on March 14, 1909, the first stadium owned by FC Barcelona was inaugurated on Calle Indústria (today called París), also known as La Escopidora. The new ground was made possible by the joint efforts of all the club's members, who helped to raise money for the stadium. It had artificial lighting from 1914, something new in Spanish stadiums at the time, as well as a never previously seen two-tiered, wooden stand built in 1916 – although it still did not have dressing rooms, which were added some time after. The seating capacity reached 1,500, with 4,500 standing.

Urban legend has it that the increasing numbers at the ground meant there was insufficient space for everyone. Consequently, scores of fans opted to sit on the upper part of the stand, showing their behinds (*cul* in Catalan) to passers-by, who jokingly started to call them *culers*. The word evolved to *culé*, which is how supporters of the *Azulgranas* (the blue and reds) are commonly and affectionately known.

It was as if the new ground exerted a lucky, magic influence. From that moment on, FC Barcelona won game after game, bringing home that year's Catalan championship trophy without losing a single match. Victories in the *Copa*

RIGHT: In 1910 a competition was staged to create the club crest that, with a few variations, is the one used today. The city's emblem had been used previously. This wooden directors' box chair, used from 1910–1922, carries an early version of the club badge.

ABOVE: Although Joan Gamper retired from playing playing football aged 25 to devote himself to his business affairs, he was president of the *Azulgranas* on five non-consecutive occasions between December 1908 and June 1925.

Pirineos Orientales – an international competition pitting Basque, Catalan and southern French teams against one another – and the *Copa de España* followed. On returning to Barcelona, after lifting the Cup in Madrid, the players were surprised by a throng of fans at the station, who had shown up to welcome the team home, the first time that this had happened. At the time, there was a drinks kiosk near the top of Las Ramblas where football results were announced. Naturally fans would visit the area to hear what was going on. And so the link between Barça and Canaletas, the name of the fountain which lends its name to that part of Las Ramblas, was forged. This is where *los culés* have been coming to celebrate their team's triumphs ever since.

After making its first appearance at the ground in March 14, 1909, the club won 13 official titles: eight Catalan championships (the last one in 1921–22) and five *Copas de España*. These were years of triumph, but also of change. The first change was the gradual disappearance of foreigners from the team, which was made up of more and more local players. Even the board saw its quota of Catalans increase. The only foreigners who remained in management were Gamper himself, president on various non-consecutive occasions until 1925, and Arthur Witty, a former player and president who was president from

1903 to 1905. Witty is credited with bringing the first regulation balls over from Britain and implementing the use of goal nets.

1910 was also the year in which the club decided to abandon the city's crest and design one of its own, by running a competition won by Santiago Femenía. The club still wears that crest today, with some minor variations: St George's cross on the left, the four stripes of the Catalan flag on the right and, in the lower part, the club's colours, blue and red, with a ball in the middle. It was a crest that would clearly define the identity of the Catalan club.

The opening season of the 1910s saw the number of members soar to 400 and the arrival of the first star players. Some of them set astounding records for the time. One such player was George Pattullo, an ex-goalkeeper turned striker. Glasgow-born Pattullo played as an amateur and arrived at Barça after Gamper himself saw him in action and convinced him to sign for the *Azulgranas*.

The Scot showed himself to be an extraordinary goalscorer, and in a single 20-game season he netted 41 goals. But there was nobody quite like Paulino Alcántara, the top goalscorer in Barcelona's history (369 goals in 357 matches) until Leo Messi took the accolade on March 16, 2014 with a hat trick.

The Philippine-born Alcántara made his debut at only 15 years of age in the 1912–13 season and his goal average was easy to calculate, one per game. He was beloved by the Barcelona fans who got accustomed to his goals, his white handkerchief hanging out of his shorts and his deceptive strength for such a slightly built man.

Although these were glory years, the club was not free from turbulence and controversy. At the start of the 1911–12 season, there was a heated meeting originally called to discuss changes to the club regulations, with which several members did not agree. Long speeches, interminable debates and even insults ensued until the founder of the club himself threatened to leave the room after uttering some harsh words: "You say that you love the club and you're killing it." The waters eventually calmed.

The issue was about money. Some players demanded salaries, and when they did not see their expectations met, refused to play in a friendly in San Sebastián. Those who played did so with such apathy that they incurred the public's wrath. The board of directors had opposed a squad petition that demanded they be paid a percentage of all money received in matches. This incident culminated in the expulsion from the team of midfielder José Quirante, who was considered the instigator

of the protest, as well as other players (the Comala and Wallace brothers, Paco Bru, Mensa and Solà) who went and founded another club, el Casual, whose existence was short-lived. Tension spread onto the pitch, and in a friendly contested by Barcelona and Espanyol, the match ended with serious incidents that caused a breakdown in relations between the two clubs.

By the 1913–14 season, foreign teams were invited to play in friendlies, and the Barcelona board invited a professional English team – Notts County – over to play for the first time. Three friendlies were played and the English team won the first two 2-0 and 4-0. The story goes that the Barcelona press, blinded by illogical pride, challenged the English players in writing that they could not score more than five goals against Barça. And so in the last match, Notts County, who initially went 3-0 down, scored ten goals in less than half an hour.

Meanwhile, away from boardroom incidents and friendlies, FC Barcelona kept winning games and racking up titles. They won the Catalan championship seven more times, and exerted absolute power until 1922, the year in which the club moved to a new stadium in Les Corts, where a new era was about to begin.

ABOVE: The first stadium owned by FC Barcelona was inaugurated on March 14, 1909 on Calle Indústria (today called París) and was financed by a joint effort from club members.

"...please allow us to warmly congratulate 'Foot-ball Club Barcelona' on commencing their sessions so promisingly."
La Vanguardia match report

BELOW: The FC Barcelona squad in 1901. Walter Wild was president at the time and the team was made up of a mix of Catalan, Swiss, English and German players. This is the first official photograph and shows (left to right, standing) Arthur Witty, Vicenç Reig, George Meyer, Pere Cabot, (in the middle row) Josep Llobet, Paul Viderkeher, Miquel Valdés, and (seated) John Parsons, Udo Steinberg, Joan Gamper, Gustavo Green and Conarre.

RIGHT: FC Barcelona used four different grounds before having its own. The first was the ex-Bonanova velodrome. The president at the time, Walter Wild, looked for a new ground after the team had to leave. FC Barcelona played their first match at the Hotel Casanovas ground (as seen in the photograph) against Hispania on November 18, 1900. The stadium was used for only one year.

ABOVE: The *Azulgranas'* president in the 1903–04 season was Barcelona-born Arthur Witty. He had British ancestry and played as a defender in the team. In just two years, the number of Catalan players had grown compared to other nationalities. Carles Comamala was the team's top scorer, with 15 goals in 12 official matches.

RIGHT: The Camp de la Indústria, where FC Barcelona played between 1909 and 1922, was popularly known as La Escopidera (the spitoon) due to its meagre dimensions.

ABOVE: The 1909–10 squad inaugurated the Camp de la Indústria, which heralded a new era, after the club had experienced a worrying drop in member numbers the previous season and was about to go out of existence. Depsite their off-the-field problems, FC Barcelona ran out winners in the Catalan and Spanish championships as well as the *Copa de los Pirineos* that season. They also won practically every friendly match.

"You say that you love the club and you're killing it."
Joan Gamper

LEFT: The French club Iris Club Lillois from Lille visited Catalonia in March 1914 and played FC Barcelona in two friendly matches. The visiting side won the first match 3-6, in a game that saw Englishman Jack Greenwell (centre) score one of Barça's consolation goals. The home showed a vast improvement in the clubs' second meeting, triumphing with an emphatic 4-1 victory.

BELOW: FC Barcelona fans queuing to enter the new Indústria ground in 1921. Such was the interest in the team, it often meant there was insufficient space to accomodate all the supporters. Scores of fans opted to sit on the upper part of the stand, showing their behinds (*cul* in Catalan) to passers-by: even today supporters are commonly known as *los culés*.

JOAN GAMPER

Although really called Hans, Gamper is affectionately known as Joan, his Catalan homonym. FC Barcelona founder Hans (or Joan) Gamper was born in 1877 in Winterthur in the Swiss canton of Zurich, where his father worked as a banker. He grew up there taking part in various sports such as cycling, athletics, swimming and, of course, football. His business aspirations led him to make Barcelona his home so he could learn Spanish, and in 1898, having just turned 20, he began to work as an accountant for the company Tranvías de Sarriá. Football was a hobby and he continued to play regularly but not competitively.

A year after arriving he published an advertisement in the magazine *Los Deportes*, calling for the formation of a football club. This was nothing new for Gamper, who had already previously founded the Excelsior football club in his native Switzerland. One month later, on November 29, 1899, with 11 fellow amateurs, Gamper officially founded a club using the name and crest of the city of Barcelona.

But Barça's historical founder did not want to be president, he just wanted to play football, and he reserved the honour of captaincy for himself, something at which he was very effective. He scored an average of two goals per game. All that needs to be said is that out of the 88 goals scored by his team in the 1901 season, 49 belonged to him. He retired from the game three years later but returned to the club in 1908, this time as president, in order to save the outfit from seemingly inevitable extinction as the number of members had fallen below 40. He was president on four other occasions, until June 1925, when an incident caused Gamper to be unable to occupy a management position ever again. These were the years of General Primo de Rivera's dictatorship and in the build-up to one match, some members of the public jeered the Spanish national anthem. The authorities ordered the closing of the ground and prohibited any type of activity by FC Barcelona for half a year. The founder, and then president, had been deposed.

His professional dealings led him to spend some years away from Barcelona and the club. It is speculated that the economic depression caused by the US stock market crash of 1929 seriously affected his business and companies. In July 1930, at 52 years of age, he took his own life. The unexpected news of his death was a bombshell in a society that had already taken the Barcelona club and turned it into a symbol of Catalan identity. The cause of his death was hidden for a long time.

Following Gamper's funeral, which was widely attended by the public, his name was engraved on a plaque in the Les Corts district. The team was still number one at that stage but it was not until 1966 that the international trophy that bears his name and is the curtain raiser for the La Liga season at the Camp Nou was introduced. Nowadays, no proud Barça member or fan would not know the founder's name, whether they choose to call him Hans or Joan.

"FC Barcelona cannot and will not die..."
Joan Gamper

2. 1920–1960: MORE THAN A CLUB

PREVIOUS PAGES: The squad for the 1924–25 season included Hungarian Platko in goal, Solà, Francesc Coma, Vicenç Piera, Samitier, Emili Sagi and Paulino Alcántara.

LEFT: Strong in the air as well being one of the best right-wingers in FC Barcelona's history, Vicente Piera "*La Bruja*" (the Witch) played for Barça 1920–33 and scored 123 goals in 395 games.

RIGHT: FC Barcelona celebrated their 25th anniversary with two matches against Real Unión de Irún on December 7 and 8, 1924, the "*Il Challenge Pere Prat*" race (an athletics competition) and the blessing of the club's flag.

During this 40-year period, Spain endured Primo de Rivera's dictatorship, the Second Spanish Republic, the Spanish Civil War and most of General Franco's regime. It was an era marked not just by sorrow, crises and all the stories that went with that but also by happiness and success for Barça, including the club's first golden era, in the 1920s. These tumultuous years created the legend of a principled, resilient club, which justly fought for its rights.

By 1920 member numbers had gradually risen to 3,000, unthinkable just a short time previously. On the pitch, Jack Greenwell, an Englishman born in Crook, County Durham, had recently been sworn in as the club's first official coach. He had arrived at Barça in 1912, to play as a midfielder. The story goes that Gamper saw him play in the Thomas Lipton Trophy (an international competition played in Turin) and persuaded him to move to Barcelona – quite a feat in an era with no television and limited international communications. It was an adventure for Greenwell, and this son of a miner distinguished himself. He retired in 1917 and it was his own team-mates who requested he become their coach. During his years at the helm, 1917–1924, Greenwell created a unit that became legendary. This was the team of Zamora, Samitier, Torralba, Martínez and Paulino Alcántara, a team that was brimming with ability and which would herald an unforgettable era, the club's first golden age.

In 1921, Joan Gamper, who had several turns as president, returned to run the club with the idea of building another more modern stadium to suit the growing status of the team and to attract more fans, who had come to appreciate a game that had been unknown just 20 years earlier. Football had become a show for ordinary people, and as a result, it was generating money and publicity. Indeed, as players became famous, their images started to appear in adverts for food and drink,

including some that were totally unsuited to sport, such as chocolate and vermouth.

In the 1921–22 season, Barça won the double by clinching both the *Campeonato de Cataluña* and *Campeonato de España* (today's *Copa Catalunya* and *Copa del Rey*), with some impressive records: out of all the matches they played, they drew two and won all the rest. And then added to this came the new ground in Les Corts. Barça were a club really going somewhere.

But the following two seasons saw the team's performance fall away, resulting in the supporters asking the board to rethink the squad. The players ended up apologizing for their poor results in a public letter. The 1924–25 season was the club's silver anniversary, marking their first 25 years. It began with Greenwell being replaced on the coaches' bench by Hungarian Jesza Poszony, under whom the club won the *Campeonato de Cataluña* and *Campeonato de España* double again.

During the 25th anniversary celebrations, Joan Gamper ended a speech, given in Catalan, with the expression "*Visca el Barça i visca Catalunya*" ("Long live Barça and long live Catalonia"). To this, the fans, congregated in Les Corts, responded with "*Visca!*", a chant which has lived on ever since,

RIGHT: The official poster for the club's 25th anniversary celebrations was designed by Josep Segrelles, an artist from Valencia. Barça had 12,207 members at the time.

heard recently from such players as Samuel Eto'o and Lionel Messi. Of course, this chant had a very particular relevance during Primo de Rivera's dictatorship. The Catalan people's freedom was severely curtailed by the government in Madrid, and although the expression was linked to a footballing celebration, it invoked pro-Catalan connotations that were obvious to all. This was the moment that FC Barcelona used sport to become associated with Catalonia. Historians and commentators have long since agreed that FC Barcelona is much more than a mere sporting symbol: it has become an entity that has allowed people to identify themselves not only with a club, but with Catalonia.

One example of this occurred during the club's silver anniversary celebrations, which took place during the dictatorship of de Rivera. De Rivera had led a military coup in 1923 and was declared Prime Minister by King Alfonso XIII. Among the measures taken by this authoritarian government was the prohibition of languages other than Spanish and a ban on certain symbols or flags, such as those of the Basque and Catalan people. During a match in honour of the Orfeó Català choir on June 14, 1925, the authorities decided to close the Barça ground after the crowd whistled during the *Marcha Real*, the Spanish national anthem. As we have seen, this incident also brought about Joan Gamper's lifetime ban from holding management positions. From December that year, the Barça presidency moved

into the hands of King Alfonso XIII's personal friend, Arcadi Balaguer, Baron Ovilvar. According to some historians, the authorities even banned people from wearing the Barça badge on their lapels – which of course made wearing it a symbol of Catalan defiance and a rejection of the regime.

From that moment on, the *"Visca el Barça"* chant was also associated with the prohibited *"Visca Catalunya"*, and the *Azulgrana* flag became a symbol of Catalan repression, replacing the beloved *señera*, the Catalonia flag. The phrase *"més que un club"* ("more than a club"), coined years later by another president, neatly sums up all this history. Throughout this time, Gamper, the Swiss who had learned to speak and write Catalan, never hid his *catalanista* allegiances.

During those years, another important layer was added to that rebellious and defiant spirit: workers who arrived in Catalonia from other regions of Spain saw expressing their affinity for a club that defended and supported Catalan freedom as a visible sign of their integration. Journalist Lluís Aymamí, a prominent Barcelona journalist (1899–1983), described this in his memoirs: "…you could not perform political acts, but football matches, which often had the same nature, were played; demonstrations were banned, but the people demonstrated en masse when they welcomed back the players after a victory outside Catalonia."

On the pitch, Barcelona kept winning titles, including the 1927–28 *Copa del Rey*. This was especially noteworthy because Barça and Real Sociedad starred in what many agree was one of the best finals ever. Two replays were needed following two 1–1 draws. The last, thrilling game saw Barça score three goals in less than 20 minutes to triumph 3–1 over Real Sociedad. Incidentally, the Les Corts pitch was now covered with grass. It had been bare earth, and was converted the previous year, at the same time as

"Gamper has been one of the steadiest mainstays in championing sport in our country. He richly deserves this tribute for his admirable work and management."
Jornada Deportiva, 1923

Romà Forns became the first Catalan (and non-foreign) manager to take charge of the team.

1928 saw the first national Spanish league championship with ten teams signed up. Barça made history by winning the inaugural competition. The title arrived after a slow start to the season with poor league results and elimination from both the *Campeonato de Cataluña* and the *Campeonato de España*. Two years later, Barça won the *Campeonato de Cataluña* but suffered their biggest ever defeat in the league against Athletic Bilbao: 12–1. At the start of the 1930–31 campaign, Joan Gamper died (it was later revealed that he had tragically taken his own life) and people went to his burial in droves to pay their respects.

THE THIRTIES: HARD TIMES AND WAR

The decade began with a new crisis and a new system of government, as the Second Spanish Republic began, on April 14, 1931. Barça once again crashed and burned against Bilbao, the "dream team" of the era, in the final of the *Campeonato de España*, although they did win the *Campeonato de Cataluña* and finished third in the national league. Member numbers dwindled and the team's style no longer excited like before.

Furthermore, during the years of the Second Republic, general interest in football decreased as greater importance was attached to political meetings and entertainment in the form of variety shows. With the loss of members, Barça's economic crisis became so acute that the club was forced to halve staff wages, although the players were still earning high salaries for the time. The squad also lost some key players, such as Piera, Sagi and especially Samitier, the great *Azulgrana* idol, who left for rivals Real Madrid. The slump reached a point where FC Barcelona were saved from relegation to the Second Division in 1934 only because the

First Division was being expanded to 12 teams for the following season.

On June 21, 1936, FC Barcelona lost the final of the *Copa de España* in Valencia against Real Madrid whose goalkeeper Zamora, an ex-*Azulgrana*, bade farewell to professional football with a legendary performance and key save in the last minute.

Less than one month later, on July 18, a group of Nationalist soldiers revolted against the Republic and civil war broke out. The first victim from Barça was its president, Josep Sunyol, a representative in Madrid of *Esquerra Republicana de Catalunya* (Republican Left of Catalonia). He was shot at the side of a road on August 6 by Franco's Nationalist troops who suspected him of carrying out politically motivated activities. Meanwhile, what people had initially thought would be a tense but short political crisis dragged on, and a climate of war gripped the nation.

Since the day the club had been founded, and as stated in the minutes from club meetings, Barcelona had offered help and assistance for people judged to need financial or political support. And so numerous people (some from the church who feared for their lives during anti-clerical assassinations) were granted refuge at the Les Corts ground. They hid there while waiting for safe passage out of the country. Neighbours from Gracia, a Barcelona district, spontaneously dedicated a road to President Sunyol, a brief tribute that disappeared at the end of the war. It would not be until 1995 that a road near the Camp Nou could be officially dedicated to him, once democracy in Spain was safely established.

During that period of uncertainty, shortages and revolutionary harangues, football clubs suffered like everyone else. Most were subject to collectivization and appropriation by worker trade unions, just as other businesses were. FC Barcelona were no exception. Given the extraordinary circumstances

| CHAPTER 2

ABOVE: José Samitier was nicknamed "the Magician" for his ability to shoot from any position. The captain of the *Azulgranas* was a prolific forward, as well as a club coach and sporting director. It was he who signed László Kubala.

and having anticipated a forced, inevitable expropriation, the club's workers took the reins and became Barça's administrators for 15 months. The hard work of men like Rossend Calvet stood out – he went on to become a club legend, fulfilling various different positions on the board.

Understandably, all sporting institutions found themselves in a fight for survival. Despite the success of the first charity matches organized by the *Azulgranas*, the reality of war gradually dampened that enthusiasm and made the club and players face up to a reality that would demand sacrifices from everybody. Some players showed much needed goodwill, giving up their bonuses or playing on after their contracts had expired, whereas others opted to seek refuge abroad, away from a country stricken by civil war, either for financial reasons or simply to try to save their own lives.

Meanwhile, member numbers were plunging, and the deteriorating economic situation led the club to make some key decisions, such as accepting an invitation to go on a sporting tour of Mexico in spring and summer 1937. This was despite the difficulties involved in taking young men, who could have been called up for military service at any moment, out of the country and committed to represent the values of a republican, democratic Spain. The tour eventually lasted five months, and on completion, 11 footballers chose not to return.

In November 1937, the special circumstances in which the club found itself ended. Once the *Comité*

de Empleados (Workers' Committee) stopped operations, the main person in charge, Francesc Xavier Casals, who had previously been on the board under presidents Sala and Suñol, was named president. Casals stayed in the post until 26 January 1939, when Barcelona was occupied by Franco's troops. His republican, trade union, democratic and *catalanista* past (he was even the Job Minister for the *Generalitat* under Macià in 1932–33) meant that reprisals were taken against him immediately by Franco's nationalist fascists and a prison sentence awaited him once the Civil War ended.

1939–60: THE YEARS OF DICTATORSHIP

Although the Civil War was now over, neither FC Barcelona's – nor the population's – problems ended. Football suffered deeply from the centralism that was generally imposed at all levels of society. The *Azulgranas* also had to tolerate the imposition of a board of directors assigned by the new authorities in Madrid. Barça's objective was to boost member numbers, as there were now little more than 3,500 left. But two years later, and despite all the problems, the 10,000-member milestone was reached. However, members and supporters had to digest the Hispanicized version of the name, *Club de Fútbol Barcelona*, and the disappearance from the club crest of two of the bar stripes from the Catalan flag.

Meanwhile, a sporting crisis in 1942 took them to the brink of relegation once again, although

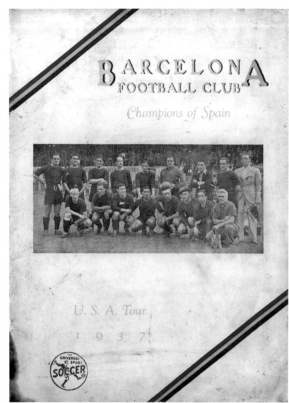

they won the *Copa del Generalísimo* – previously the *Copa de España* and the competition today called the *Copa del Rey*. This was the decade of César Rodriguez, one of the greatest goalscorers in the club's history; legendary winger Basora; goalkeeper Ramallets; and coach de Samitier, who won the first league title in 15 years in 1944–45. It was also the start of the heated rivalry with Real Madrid, both on a sporting and socio-political level, thanks to a match *los culés* call the "scandal of Chamartín" – and which *los madridistas* remember as the day they put 11 goals past Barça at Real Madrid's home stadium Charmartin.

The match in question was the second leg of the 1943 cup semi-final. FC Barcelona had won the first leg 3–0 at Les Corts against a team that was starting to be seen in Catalonia as one that identified themselves with Franco's regime. The atmosphere was therefore unusually hostile for the visitors. Although there are different versions of events that day, the testimonies from the players present all agree on the following:

- the Madrid press hyped the event as never before;
- the Barça supporters' journey to the capital was blocked for fear of riots;
- each Chamartín attendee received a whistle on entry, to goad the visitors;
- referee Celestino Rodríguez went to the *Azulgrana* dressing room before the game to instruct them to lose, after a security

representative had told him in unsubtle terms, "Look at what's happening on the terraces. We cannot allow anything to happen here. You already know what you have to do";
- when the players refused to continue playing in the second half because of the constant rain of objects thrown at them, an army colonel entered the Barça dressing room and threatened to arrest the team if they did not go back out onto the pitch.

Barça ended up conceding 18 goals, seven of which were ruled out. Goalkeeper Miró retired from football because of the match.

GOLDEN ANNIVERSARY

Before welcoming in the 1950s, five more pieces of silverware were added to the trophy cabinet, including two successive league titles and one *Copa Latina*, the precursor to the European Cup, their first European title. The coach at the time was Enrique Fernández, who had played for Barça before the Civil War. He advocated an attacking style of football, which would see the team scoring freely in most games. FC Barcelona was in fine fettle as it turned 50 years old, in 1949.

The club celebrated this anniversary with almost 25,000 members and a respectable list of honours: four leagues, nine cups and 22 Catalan championships. They took advantage of the occasion to restore the four stripes they lost after the war. A legendary squad approached the new decade: César, Biosca, Basora, Gonzalvo III, Segarra,

ABOVE LEFT: The club decided that the *Azulgrana* flag would fly at half-mast to honour Gamper, who had died on July 30, 1930. Some players carry the coffin on their shoulders during his widely attended funeral procession in Barcelona.

ABOVE: The US tour in 1937 provided a substantial injection of money and allowed Barça to act as ambassadors for the Spanish Republic. Emilio Marrese tells the story in his book *Rosa de fuego*.

Moreno, Manchón, Ramallets and a new signing, Hungarian László Kubala. This is the team that won four *Ligas*, five *Copas de España*, one *Copa Latina*, two *Copas de Feria* (the precursor to the UEFA Cup) and two *Copas Eva Duarte* (the precursor to today's *Supercopa*) in the space of a decade.

Of course, the season that all *barcelonistas* of a certain age remember is the "five *Copas*" in 1952. It was the crowning moment for a Barcelona team touched by the unusual talent of Kubala, who arrived in 1950, and the special group of players around him. Barça maintained supremacy the following season, with an attractive, fresh and efficient style influenced by techniques introduced by the prodigious Hungarian. The popularity of games at Les Corts stadium led to over-capacity crowds, which the stadium struggled to cope with.

The attractive playing style shown by the team led by Kubala, along with the country's economic recovery, saw member numbers gradually increase to 52,791 in 1960. Everything pointed towards continued growth, especially when the club decided to sign another star to complete their legendary frontline, Argentinian Alfredo Di Stefano. This became the most controversial signing in the history of Spanish football. The player had left River Plate for Millonarios de Bogotá, and was sought after by Real Madrid, too. Both teams claimed to have the rights and pertinent permission for his signature, but the case was so complicated that it ended with a wise solution from the *Delegación Nacional de Deportes Española* (the Spanish National Sports' Delegation): the Argentinian would play for both clubs. The licence necessary to play professionally would be shared between the two and he would switch between the teams each season, starting with Real Madrid. Barça rejected that option and waived their rights over signing the player, an act underlined by the resignation of *Azulgrana* president, Enric Martí Carreto.

There are differing versions of what actually happened, but it is undeniable that external agents, obstructive tactics, nonsensical attitudes, and all types of rumour-mongering and pressure were involved. The issue even became a matter of state importance, and the signing of foreign footballers was prohibited. The "Blond Arrow", who had already played some friendlies for Barça, stayed at Real Madrid.

It was inevitable that the decree banning foreign players had to be amended. Those who were already in negotiations to come to Spain before the rule was implemented had to be recognized. The Falangist newspaper *Arriba* wrote about the incident in its subsequent report: "The *Delegación de Deportes* has shown it knows how to interpret the unanimous feeling that all sport-loving Spaniards have." The interim committee in charge of managing Barça after Martí Carreto's resignation signed a document on October 23, 1953, clearing the way for the player to join Real Madrid, in return for the *Azulgranas* receiving compensation to the tune of four million pesetas. At that moment, Barcelona's supremacy was ended by their most direct rival.

But one year later, in 1954, Barça signed an extraordinary player of their own – Luis Suárez, still the only Spanish player to have won the *Ballon d'Or*, in 1960, while an FC Barcelona player. Off the pitch, work began on a new stadium promised by president Miró-Sans. It was inaugurated in September 1957 with an initial capacity of 93,053. This new temple for *barcelonismo*, the Camp Nou, was later expanded to accommodate 98,772 spectators, making it the biggest footballing arena in Europe. Before the end of the decade, a new coach appeared: Helenio Herrera, the man who gave Barça back its title as a competitive and victorious outfit by winning *La Liga* in 1959 and 1960, *La Copa de España* in 1958 and the Fairs Cup in 1960.

RIGHT: László Kubala during a league match against Jaén (January 20, 1957) which Barça won 4–2, with goals by Manchón, Basora and Suárez (who scored two).

ABOVE: On February 25, 1923, a tribute match to Gamper was held involving players from all Catalan clubs (except Espanyol and Europa), and some Spanish and European ones, too. FC Barcelona beat the Catalan XI 2–1 in front of 25,000 spectators.

BELOW: Barça win their sixth *Copa del Rey* on May 10, 1925. After a mini-league made up of the various regional champions, FC Barcelona faced Club Arena de Getxo at the Estadio Reina Victoria de Sevilla, running out 2–0 winners with goals by J. Samitier and A. Sancho.

RIGHT: FC Barcelona won the first Spanish league championship, which began in February 1929. Over the four-and-a-half-month long campaign, Barça won 11, drew 3 and lost 4 of the 18 matches (20 fewer than nowadays). Real Madrid finished second, two points off the champions' tally of 25.

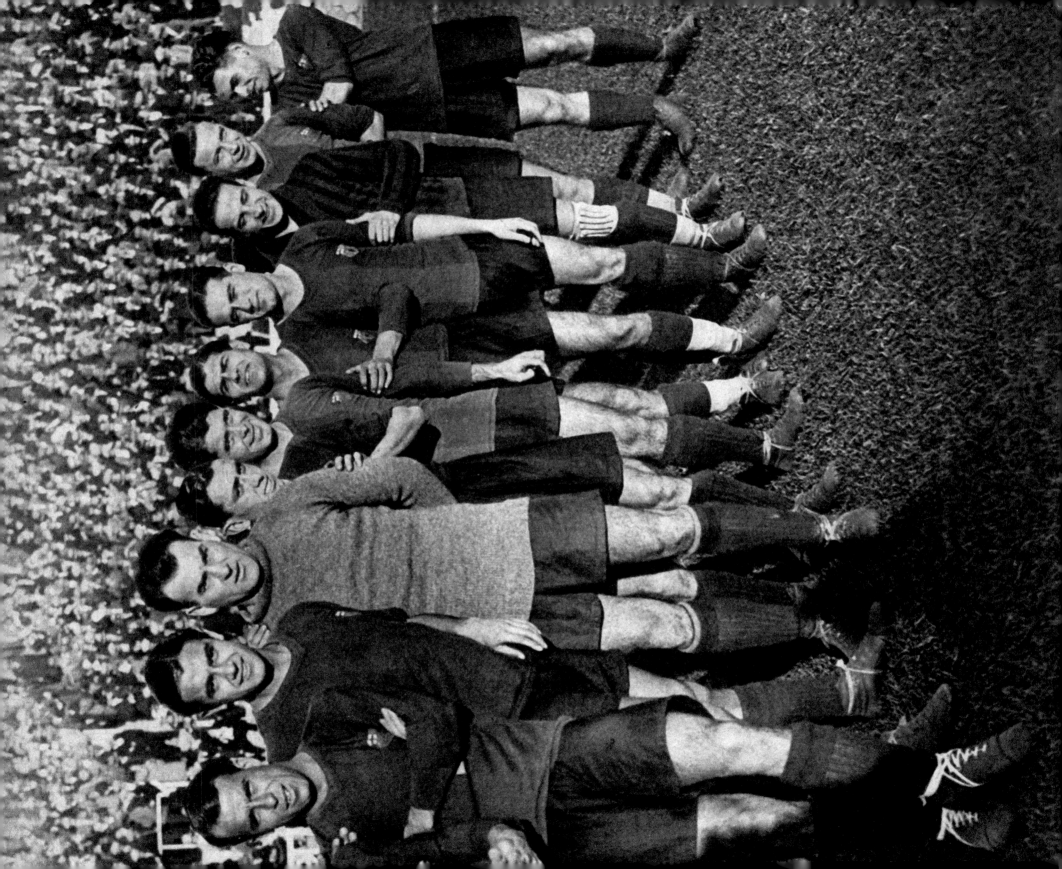

ABOVE: Barça's attack in the 1920s boasted players such as Vicente Piera, an exceptional right-winger who came up through the club's youth system. He made his first-team debut as a replacement for the injured Paulino Alcántara. The two goals he scored that day helped him become a first-team player at Barça.

RIGHT: Forward César Rodríguez, one of the club's top goalscorers. He won five *Ligas*, three *Copas de España* and two *Copas Latinas* between 1942 and 1955.

LEFT: Forward Mariano Martin, known as "the Aerial Force". His average of more than a goal per game made him the first *Pichichi* (league top scorer) in *Azulgrana* colours in the 1941–42 season.

BELOW: László Kubala receives plaudits from supporters at the Les Corts ground after scoring a goal in Barça's title-winning 1951–52 campaign.

ABOVE LEFT: On March 28, 1954, the first brick was laid of what would become FC Barcelona's new stadium. The inaugural match was against a Warsaw team on September 24, 1957, which the *Azulgranas* won 4–2. The first Barça goal at the ground was scored by Eulogio Martínez.

BELOW LEFT: The name Camp Nou became popular in opposition to the old Les Corts ground, although the first option was "Joan Gamper", rejected by the authorities at the time. The first official match was played on October 6, 1957, against Real Jaén. Barça ran out 6–1 winners.

BELOW: Luis Suárez played for FC Barcelona between 1954 and 1961. The man nicknamed "the Golden Galician" due to his roots and "the Architect" due to his vision on the pitch was a left-sided midfielder blessed with various qualities. His excellent technique, ability on the ball, creativity and finishing saw him become the first and only Spaniard to date to win the *Ballon d'Or* in 1960. His most exceptional years were arguably spent at Helenio Herrera's Inter, having left Barça for a world record transfer fee at the time, because of the dire financial situation in which the *Azulgranas* found themselves.

LÁSZLÓ KUBALA

Kubala was born in Budapest, Hungary, in 1927 and arrived in Barcelona in 1950, already a renowned player in his home country. He had left Hungary two years prior to his arrival in Spain, for ideological and financial reasons. He was opposed to the Hungarian communist regime and was in search of a club that could offer him protection as a player, as well as higher economic remuneration.

A complaint to FIFA from his previous team Vasas SC earned him a footballing suspension, so in the meantime he temporarily played for Aurora Pro Patria in Busto Arsizio, Italy. Alongside other exiled players from Central Europe, he was a part of the unofficial Hungary squad, a team that was without a football federation and which played friendly matches all over Europe. They were managed by Kubala's brother-in-law, Ferdinand Daučík, who would later coach the *Azulgranas* as part of the agreement signed with Kubala.

It was during one such fixture against Espanyol that Josep Samitier, then FC Barcelona technical director, spotted him and started to move heaven and earth to sign him. The fact that Kubala was a refugee who had fled a communist country went down well with the right-wing Spanish authorities, who not only supported Barça's attempt to sign him by pulling strings with FIFA but also supplied the player with Spanish citizenship.

From Day One, the forward displayed a series of astounding techniques, then unknown to the Spanish players. His shots from set pieces were struck with the inside of the foot, creating so much swerve that opposition goalkeepers could not read them and were left floundering.

His effortless ball control allowed him to develop extraordinary vision, and to these skills he added dribbling, shooting and precise penalty-taking.

He helped Barça win the 1951 *Copa de España* and his goalscoring statistics from the following season included seven goals in one game against Sporting de Gijón, a 9–0 victory (a joint record for most goals in a single league game, shared with Athletic de Bilbao's Agustín Sauto "Bata", who achieved the same feat in a 12–1 win over Barcelona in 1930–31); five goals against Celta de Vigo; and two hat tricks out of the 14 which he netted during his stay at Barcelona. Today he is still one of the club's top goalscorers.

Kubala was stocky and physically very strong, so he knew how to protect the ball. However, he deteriorated physically as injuries, mainly caused by strong tackles by opposition defenders, took their toll on him. In 1952–53, he managed to overcome a bronchial illness that was threatening to end his career.

He retired as a player in 1961 and returned to the club as a coach a few months later, until 1963. He would later coach the Spanish national team from 1969 until 1980. He died in Barcelona on May 17, 2002. In 2009, a statue was erected at the Camp Nou to honour this legendary figure.

"They all have their merits, each to their own. But for me, there's nobody quite like Kubala."
From the *Kubala* song (1989) by J.M. Serrat

3. 1960–1988: MICHELS, CRUYFF AND MARADONA

3. **1960–1988: MICHELS, CRUYFF AND MARADONA**

This period in FC Barcelona's history spans almost three decades, from the 1960s to the end of the 1980s. The name of this footballing institution had already been changed to the more Spanish and patriotic *Club de Fútbol Barcelona* in accordance with the times, which were dominated by an oppressive dictatorship.

The 1960s saw the club go through a period of minimal success on the pitch but unparalleled growth in member numbers. This curious phenomenon can be explained by focusing on the club's social aspect. In those years, sport became one of the few accepted ways for repressed Catalan citizens to protest in public: sports associations were allowed to meet, a relative freedom that did not apply to most other activities. FC Barcelona's strong commitment to *catalanismo* and democracy, expressed years earlier during the previous dictatorship in the Second Republic and even the Civil War, was vital for people who wanted to identify with the struggle against an imposed and unfair regime. It was through sport that people vented their anger, particularly in Catalonia and other communities around Spain whose cultures were being repressed.

It must not be forgotten that in that same period a large number of people from other parts of the country arrived in Catalonia. It is estimated that the Catalan population grew in that decade by 1.2 million people, all of whom were looking for work and for a stability that had been denied them in other parts of Spain. Barça once again became a place for integration, just as it had been in the 1920s and 1930s. The new arrivals may not have even spoken Catalan or known the local customs, but shouting *"Visca el Barça!"* from the terraces made it easier for them not only to be accepted by Catalan society but also to feel part of it. This was important because the majority of the new members were working-class, principally the sons of Civil War veterans who had found themselves on the losing side. They were able to recognize a model of strength and resolution in FC Barcelona in the face of the abuse of power by the ultra-conservative, centralized regime.

This was also the decade that saw television gradually enter the homes of Spanish families, taking football into the living rooms of those who could afford sets for the first time. Others had to make do with going to a bar, to a neighbour or relative's house or crowding in front of shop windows, a very common sight in those days.

THE GENERATION GAP

The flying 50s came to an end with Helenio Herrera and a magnificent generation of players, led by Kubala, firing on all cylinders. But the *Azulgranas* did not make a good start to the next decade, losing to Real Madrid in the European Cup semi-finals. Barça had managed to get their hands on the 1959–60 league title, but losing out in Europe seemed to bring the club misfortune, and not only in sporting terms. To start with, during the championship celebrations, some players started to demand higher bonuses for future victories at a time when the club's finances were under strain because of the costs involved in building the recently opened Camp Nou and the ongoing increases in player wages and bonuses. The atmosphere in the squad became strained, which contributed to Real Madrid winning both legs 3–1.

This defeat, coupled with the rest of the off-the-field episodes, led the board to dispose of Herrera in 1960, and for the following season to install Yugoslav Ljubiša Broćić, the former coach of his country's national team. But he lasted only a few games. The team did not gel and the board decided to install Broćić 's advisor at the time, Oriazola, who was also unable to generate decent performances from an ageing squad.

PREVIOUS PAGES: Johan Cruyff scores against Atlético de Madrid on December 22, 1973. The following day the press defined the goal as "impossible" and supporters baptized the player "the Flying Dutchman".

LEFT: Barça's Peruvian star Hugo Sotil scoring against Real Madrid in the historic 5–0 at the Bernabéu on February 17, 1974. "El Cholo" headed home a Cruyff cross from the right, after earning a free kick. It was the fifth on a jubilant evening.

OVERLEAF: Evaristo's legendary header, which eliminated Real Madrid from the European Cup last 16 in 1960–61. An iconic image of *barcelonismo*.

RIGHT: 1. FC Köln, Anderlecht and Nantes participated in the inaugural Joan Gamper Trophy in 1966. FC Barcelona ran out winners after defeating FC Köln 3–1 in the final with Josep Maria Fusté, Joaquim Rifé and Luis Vidal scoring a goal each for the Catalans.

The talent previously displayed by the team was gradually waning as the players neared the end of their careers and could no longer produce performances like before.

This decline meant that the team finished fourth in *La Liga* in 1960–61, a staggering 20 points behind champions Real Madrid, and was eliminated from the *Copa del Rey*. The only heroic moment of the season arrived in the shape of Evaristo's goal against Real Madrid in the European Cup round of 16. Images of the *Azulgrana* player's diving header were seen the world over. Barça reached the final, but lost 3–2 to Lisbon's Benfica, including an own goal by Ramallets, one of Barça's best-ever goalkeepers.

The poor results led to president Miró-Sans's inevitable resignation and the new board decided to sell Luis Suárez to Inter Milan for 25m pesetas (€2.2m) at the end of that season, before the next presidential election. At the time, this was the most expensive transfer in history. Economic need dictated the sale, but in sporting terms the transfer would be regretted because Suárez continued to play magnificently at other clubs.

On June 7, 1961 incoming president Enric Llaudet arrived at a club with a debt of 284m pesetas, an excessive one at the time. He even proposed in a referendum the possible sale of the Les Corts ground. The club's season ticket holders decided not to sell, but the need to generate funds remained an issue.

Suárez was not the only big loss in the 1961–62 season. Czibor left for Espanyol, Tejada went to Real Madrid and both Kubala and goalkeeper Ramallets retired. Kubala's last game was at the Camp Nou in August 1961, a friendly in which his friends Di Stefano and Puskás also wore the *Azulgrana* shirt.

This golden era was over, and gave way to years that were more like wandering in the wilderness. Ex-*Azulgrana* goalkeeper Lluís Miró started out at the helm, but Kubala would inherit his team by Matchday 14 after the former resigned, furious at the players' attitude on the pitch during a 6–2 annihilation away to Valencia. Miró, *culé* to the core, accused the squad of making fools of themselves and not knowing how to wear the shirt with honour. His replacement, Kubala, plus the impact on the players after Miró's dressing-down, made the team shoot up the league and eventually finish second. The team also reached the Fairs Cup final, which would be played at the start of the following season. Once again, their opponents were Valencia. And once again, they lost 6–2 in the first leg. The tie was effectively over.

Lack of funds prevented the signing of great players, but even so members had the feeling that the players were not giving their all. Kubala also suffered the indignity of a mid-season dismissal, in January 1963, with Barça in mid-table obscurity and out of the Fairs Cup. This also spelled the end of the football school set up by Kubala under the guidance of the president, Llaudet. Barça saved face by winning the *Copa del Rey* in a final against Zaragoza, unusually played at the Camp Nou because Franco was visiting Catalonia at the time. Credit for the win went to the coach who replaced Kubala, Josep Gonzalvo.

The financial situation was slowly correcting itself, with lower player wages easing the burden on the club's coffers. It was on that note that Barça began the 1963 league season with César Rodríguez as coach. A forward from the 1940s and 50s, he inherited a squad seemingly lacking in tenacity, whose best players, such as Kocsis and Segarra, were the wrong side of 30. However, he ran into a president who was reluctant to buy new blood, because too many players had been bought who failed to fit in.

ABOVE: The phrase *"més que un club"* is owed to Narcís de Carreras, who was declared FC Barcelona president on January 17, 1968. It would later become the club's motto.

Despite these restrictions, César managed to build a free-scoring team that had a chance of winning the *La Liga* title, but Real Madrid topped them by four points, which Barça had dropped in the two *clásicos* that season. The supporters were disillusioned by a team that for some time had been offering occasional sublime performances and many goals, but no trophies. Member numbers fluctuated throughout the season, though the importance of being associated with Barça meant that on average member numbers increased by 1,000 per year.

The non-sporting connotations of being affiliated with FC Barcelona started to weigh on the players' minds and they had to endure all sorts of insults, then more uncommon and disproportionate, as they travelled around Spain.

The year began with Espanyol making their rivals an unprecedented offer: faced with Barça's refusal to sell them the Les Corts ground for economic reasons, they suggested renting the Camp Nou on Sundays when it was not needed by the *Azulgranas*. Barça turned them down, of course.

A new season began with César at the helm, but only until the fifth matchday, given the poor results. In fact, the board's unhappiness with the coach and players' performances was such that after a 5–1 thrashing by lowly Levante, it imposed a fine on the whole squad, complaining that "the team's woeful performance does not correspond in any way to the players' professional category, our club's prestige and its mass of supporters." César resigned with immediate effect.

There was little that the newly appointed coach Vicenç Sasot could do. Particularly because the team's poor play was accompanied by bad luck. A key example was the tie against RC Strasbourg. After getting through two Fairs Cup knockout rounds to reach the quarter-finals in 1964–65, Barça drew 0–0 on three occasions, including the

decider, so the tie was decided by the referee's coin toss. Barça lost.

In spite of everything, president Llaudet was re-elected through the old voting system, in which only the votes of certain members counted. His re-election may have been because the bad performances were attributed to the players; Llaudet was thanked for his tight control of the club's economic reins.

At the halfway point of this mediocre decade, the president approved the signing of new players renowned throughout Spanish football and was about to close a deal to sell the Les Corts ground. Carlex Rexach had made his debut the previous season, having come up through the ranks at Condal, FC Barcelona's B team, which had been founded in 1934 as *Sección Deportiva La España Industrial*, and renamed *Club Deportivo Condal* 22 years later. Condal had spent the last nine years of its existence in the Third Division, with the exception of two seasons in the second tier. In 1970, the team merged with Atlètic Catalunya to form a new club, FC Barcelona B, the Barça reserves.

The Argentinian coach, Roque Olsen, did not select Rexach for a single game that season, however. Lluís Pujol, also from Condal, enjoyed more luck and played two league and four Fairs Cup games. He found the net six times, a respectable return. Olsen got it wrong with Rexach, reaching the conclusion that he had no chance of succeeding at Barça. His team did not manage to bring home *La Liga* or *La Copa*, but did win the Fairs Cup because this time luck was on FC Barcelona's side: the coin tossed in the air to decide the tie against Hannover went the way of Olsen's men. The semi-final against Chelsea was a very tight encounter, although Barça comfortably won the replay 5–0. So the season ended on a high note, from winning the 1965–66 Fairs Cup against Zaragoza and by pocketing the

> *"Those who say I do not love Catalonia are incorrect. I love and admire it, despite the Catalans."*
> **Santiago Bernabéu**

226m pesetas (€27m) earned from selling the Les Corts ground.

The board, headed by Llaudet, approved the creation of a trophy named after the club's founder. And so, the 1966–67 season saw the inauguration of the Joan Gamper Trophy, which has been the pre-season curtain-raiser ever since. FC Barcelona won that first tournament, which settled a long-standing debt of gratitude to the Swiss man. But this win was the highlight of a season filled with more woes than glory. The defence of the previous season's Fairs Cup, which was won against Zaragoza in September 1966, failed at the first hurdle as Dundee United ran out 4–1 winners on aggregate. Barça reached second in the league, but it was not enough, and the fans waved their white handkerchiefs at the end of each match to display their frustration with the team's performances, and the board.

As was becoming the norm, all these sporting problems did not cause member numbers to fall – in fact, quite the opposite. Many fans got accustomed to a losing Barça side, which may be the origin of that *culé* caution, or pessimism, which strikes before the end of a match, even when the team is winning.

Former Barcelona player Salvador Artigas became the club's new coach for 1967–68. During the Civil War, he had been a pilot for the Republicans, which is why he spent some time in France in exile. Hiring him was one of Llaudet's final actions as president at a time when his leadership was questioned by the rest of the board. Although the team was not firing on all cylinders, they still seemed to be coping well in *La Liga*, until the sudden death of *Azulgrana* player Julio César Benítez one day before the *clásico*, which left the team lifeless. The *clásico* was postponed by a few days and the

barcelonistas just about scraped a draw but then lost momentum in the league, eventually finishing second.

In the elections for a new president, Narcís de Carreras got the nod. He was a relevant, public figure, who had adapted to the dictatorial period with a certain stoicism and had had more than a few problems with the authorities. Carreras, a long-term member, had already been club secretary in the 1950s and knew the ins and outs of Barça as well as its identity and history. Maybe this is how he ended up writing a single, throwaway phrase in his inaugural address, which would not only have a huge impact but would remain the club's motto forever. On 17 January 1968, Carreras read his speech, emphasizing for the first time that FC Barcelona was *"més que un club"* ("more than a football club"). The phrase stuck, so much so that it has lasted until today as the defining philosophy of the *Azulgrana*s.

That season ended with another altercation between FC Barcelona and Real Madrid during another final for the *Generalísimo* cup, played in the capital. The Catalans emerged victorious thanks to an own goal by defender Zunzunegui in the seventh minute. Minutes later the Madrid fans started protesting about the referee's decisions, considering him to be pro-*barcelonista*. The atmosphere became especially heated after a Madrid penalty appeal was turned down and the crowd reacted by "reprehensibly throwing bottles onto the field of play, a heavy rain of projectiles", as reported by newspaper *ABC*. The report added, in the rhetoric of the time, that football "is a constant democracy, with the principal danger that the votes are sometimes wildly deposited in bottles which are thrown onto the field of play, like messages are thrown into the sea." From that

day onwards entry to stadiums with glass bottles was prohibited.

The rivalry between Real Madrid and Barça is natural. These two renowned clubs are from Spain's two most important cities, each with its own sporting, social and political differences. But at this tense time, the Real Madrid president, Santiago Bernabéu, stoked the fire by making some controversial statements to a sports' newspaper. Bernabéu, a conservative who fought on Franco's side for the Spanish Nationalists, said: "Those who say I do not love Catalonia are incorrect. I love and admire it, despite the Catalans." The impact of that interview was monumental. Not even the authorities approved, fearful of cementing the Catalonia–Barça link forever.

The following season (1968–69) was disastrous for FC Barcelona. They finished third in *La Liga*, 11 points behind Real Madrid; lost 3–2 to Slovan Bratislava in the Cup Winners' Cup Final; and lost their president, Carreras, who was worn down by internal politics. The winner of the subsequent elections was Agustí Montal Jnr, a man linked to previous boards. He was vice-president with Carreras and a known *catalanista* supporter – to a much greater extent than he was able to show in public at the time. Meanwhile, three coaches arrived and left the club without any of them putting an end to the poor run of form: Barça finished fourth in *La Liga* in 1969–70, after being in much lower positions in the table, and said goodbye to both the Fairs Cup and *Copa del Generalísimo* in the quarter-finals.

The latter was against Real Madrid and involved a new scandal involving a referee whose name was remembered for a long time: Guruceta. Barcelona had to come back from a 2–0 loss in the first leg at the Bernabéu. However, it was the controversial refereeing decisions that the *culé* public and large sections of the press were more interested in.

The lead journalist chronicling the event for daily newspaper *ABC* wrote about "a match that was more akin to a bad crime show than a sporting event". He was writing about events that began in the 59th minute, when Guruceta awarded a penalty to Madrid for a foul committed outside the penalty area. At the time, Barcelona were leading 1–0. Now all hell broke loose. In the words of the *ABC* journalist,

Faced with such a glaring error, the crowd reacted furiously, venting their anger in various ways … The Azulgrana *captain Eladio applauded sarcastically. Mr Guruceta gave him his marching orders with such an abrasive and authoritative gesture that when he put out his arm to show him the way to the dressing rooms, he inadvertently struck Grosso, who fell to the ground. Then back to more arguments, protests and the embarrassing spectacle as the Barcelona players tried to leave the pitch en masse. Seats were raining onto the pitch.*

The match eventually resumed and was teeming with incident, the most serious of which was that the final whistle was blown early, after the ball disappeared into the crowd and the pitch was covered in cushions and invading fans. The result of the chaos was that Barça were eliminated from the Cup, received the maximum fine of 90,000 pesetas and were ordered to close the stadium, the referee was suspended for six months and the head of the referees' association resigned.

Barça had to wait until the opening season of the following decade, the 1970s, for British coach Vic Buckingham to bring home *La Copa* for the *Azulgranas,* against Valencia. *La Liga* slipped out of their grasp thanks to Valencia's superior head-to-head record, leaving Barça second. Buckingham then had to leave his post

> *"...constantly harassing the adversary, not even giving him time to breathe in order to recover possession as well as not relinquishing the attacking initiative to your opponent at any cost."*
> **Rinus Michels**

due to illness after finally managing to achieve consistent team performances. This much-needed stability seemed to have been lost again. But then Dutchman Rinus Michels took over the reins. And a new era began.

THE 1970S: MICHELS AND CRUYFF
As a sign of the changing times, FC Barcelona started the decade by publishing the editorial for its internal newsletter in Catalan, a language that was still officially banned. The use of Catalan was gradually extended to some articles and also appeared on some on membership cards. In an act of bravery, the club also began using the language for stadium announcements, although this was immediately stopped by the authorities. Meanwhile, Barça as a sporting institution was growing and, in 1971, the club inaugurated new facilities at Palau Blaugrana, for the basketball, handball and roller hockey teams, as well as an ice rink.

With Michels at the helm, the team ended the season well by adding the Fairs Cup to the trophy cabinet. A new competition under the name of the UEFA Cup was to be launched the following year, so the last and original Fairs Cup was played for in a one-off match between Barça, the first winners and the team who had won the competition a record three times, and Leeds United, the 1970–71 winners. Barcelona would triumph in this one-off match 2–1 thanks to two Dueñas goals.

The team started the 1970–71 league season badly and even found themselves sixteenth in the table in late November. However, halfway through the campaign, the tactics introduced by "Mr Marble", as the new coach was nicknamed, started to bear fruit and the team ended up third.

The Dutchman, who had arrived at Barça after winning everything at Ajax, inherited a team in need of some discipline, which he had no qualms about instilling. He is remembered today as the inventor of "total football", but his tactics did not start to produce results until the arrival of another Dutchman, Johan Cruyff. Michels himself defined what he called pressing football:

> *It involves constantly harassing the adversary, not even giving him time to breathe in order to recover possession as well as not relinquishing the attacking initiative to your opponent at any cost. It relies on two basic requirements: an unbreakable fighting spirit and perfect physical preparation, without which the system inevitably collapses.*

Under Michels, the players learned how to be versatile and constantly press the opposition. They kept the ball at all times and also looked to attack at every opportunity, which generated excitement among the supporters. "Total football" is now known the world over but, at the time, nobody had thought that a forward could defend or a defender could attack. His philosophy had worked at Ajax, but initially there were doubts that it could be exported.

Barcelona had been in pole position for most of the 1971–72 and 1972–73 seasons, but did not end up champions, tailing off towards the end. The Cup loss to second division Sevilla in the last 16 is still remembered. The press referred to a tired and lifeless team, and Michels gave the players a stern telling-off when he caught them making a toast with cava in the hotel after the game. Subsequently, the board decided to fine the players.

1972 was the year of the "false natives case" which facilitated the return of foreign players to Spanish clubs – foreign players had been banned since 1962. The only foreigners allowed to play in Spain then were "natives", descendants of Spaniards born outside the country. This limitation caused many clubs to end up on the wrong side of

LEFT: In May 1973, new legislation came into force allowing clubs to sign foreign players after years of restrictions in this regard. Dutchman Johan Cruyff (left) and Peruvian Hugo Sotil (right) were able to sign for Barça.

the law when signing players who claimed that their parents were born in places such as Osasuna, Celta or Betis. A scandal over foreign signings broke out because Barça had the guts to kick up a fuss.

The team's management had wanted to make the Paraguayan Irala a national for some time, but the Spanish federation did not allow it, arguing that he had already represented his country at international level. But the federation was showing clear bias since it had allowed other players in the same situation to play for other Spanish clubs. So the Barcelona board, headed by Monta, hired a team of lawyers, who proved that a large number of those players (46 out of 60) had fake documents.

The scandal had entailed the participation of consulates and embassies, along with other authorities, making it such a significant issue that the club showed the results from the investigation to the Royal Spanish Football Federation in private. Agreement was reached not to make the results public if the signing of foreign players was made possible. The new legislation came into force in May 1973, allowing each team to sign two foreigners. Barça signed Hugo Sotil and Johan Cruyff.

1973–74: A SEASON OF EMOTIONS

Although Cruyff signed in August 1973, bureaucratic obstacles meant that he did not make his debut until eight games into the season, against Granada, on October 28. Five games later and Barça, under Michels' orders and with their most accomplished disciple leading the line, found themselves on top of the league, a position they would not relinquish all season. The Camp Nou was finally able to celebrate a title triumph after a 14-year drought, the league won with brilliant football that was both attractive and effective.

It would prove to be an emotional season: there was Cruyff's arrival, the league title after so many years, the restoration of the club's original name

and the 5–0 win at the Bernabéu that gave way to the 75th anniversary celebrations the following year. Much has been written about that 5–0 victory over Madrid, almost all of which echoes the comments of an *ABC madridista* reporter, who described the Barcelona team that season as being "as finely tuned as a piano can be under Arthur Rubinstein's prodigious fingers".

To commemorate the club's 75th anniversary, a group of "universal Catalans" (as they were called) was formed, to contribute their talents. Painter Joan Miró designed the anniversary poster, while Josep Maria Espinàs and Jaume Picas's text was used for lyrics to the *Cant del Barça*, which was invented for the occasion and almost immediately became the official anthem. Some 3,500 voices, from 78 choirs present at the Camp Nou, sang it for the first time on the day of the commemorative celebrations, before the match against East Germany on November 27, 1974. Its lyrics bring together those values for which Barça like to be recognized:

- Unity – "it does not matter where we come from, be it the south or the north";
- Integration – "a flag connects us";
- The team – "we have a name, everyone knows it";
- The sense of being more than a club – "Barça, Barça, Baaaarça."

On the back of this wave of emotion, Montal stood for re-election and won with an overwhelming majority. He even printed propaganda material with Carrera's motto "Barça is more than a club", but this was never used.

The following season, 1974–75, looked promising thanks in part to two new additions: defender Migueli from Ceuta, who had debuted the previous year; and Johan Neeskens, another Dutchman who had arrived to strengthen the midfield. Yet, against all predictions, the

> *"Barcelona [under the then relatively unknown Terry Venables] showed they're an unrivalled team. They topped the table from start to finish, dominating the competition."*
> **Sport**

RIGHT: After signing a contract with FC Barcelona on June 4, 1982, Maradona declared: "I feel excited. I think I've signed for a marvellous club, one which has excited me for a long time. I'll give Barcelona my best."

FAR RIGHT: Although he had hepatitis and suffered a serious injury, there were brilliant moments during his two seasons as an *Azulgrana*, such as the goals against Red Star Belgrade in the Cup Winners' Cup and Real Madrid in the *Copa de la Liga* in 1983.

wheels set in motion just one campaign earlier started to come off. After a good start, the team gradually went off track, and Barcelona were only seventh after 17 games. They made a recovery but still finished third, 13 points behind Real Madrid. They did not enjoy any success in the Cup either, with Zaragoza eliminating them in the quarter-finals, and the team then came up short in the European Cup semi-finals against Leeds United. The board decided to show Michels the door and brought in German Hennes Weissweiler for the coming season.

Politically, Spain was experiencing its last year under Franco's regime. The dictator was on his death bed and in October temporarily relinquished power to Prince Juan Carlos. However, his government still had time to carry out five of their 11 planned executions in September 1975, which generated a storm of international protest. When Franco finally died on November 20, 1975, FC Barcelona published a newsletter in which the club bluntly declared its support for the country's transition to democracy. Hardly one month later, on December 28, 1975, Madrid visited the Camp Nou, where huge numbers of *Señera* flags could be seen for the first time in years. These were brought into the stadium secretly for a match that would be televised, making this a great opportunity for Barça's supporters to express their *catalanista* feelings. Just to add to the excitement, it was all square until the last minute, when Rexach scored the winning goal for Barça.

But the team's performances were still inconsistent and the arguments between Cruyff and Weissweiler became more and more heated until the latter resigned in early April. He was replaced internally by a man who was achieving success with the youth teams, Laureano Ruíz. It was too late to make up lost ground in the league, however, and Barça ended the season five points from top spot.

Rinus Michels's comeback in 1976–77 brought renewed hope to the *culé* supporters. The first league match was broadcast on the radio in Catalan for the first time since the end of the Civil War. This was a campaign packed full of goals, but even so the team finished second – only one point behind champions Atlético de Madrid but second, nonetheless. Bilbao eliminated Barça from the UEFA Cup, leaving the trophy cabinet empty for another year.

A home match against Malaga on Matchday 21 stands out as controversial with disruption caused by an out-of-control minority. The match would be remembered for aggression against the referee and chaotic scenes including a vehicle belonging to TVE, Television Espanola, being set on fire.

Málaga were awarded a goal that was both offside and a handball, and Barça were denied two stone-wall penalties. Cruyff was sent off and later suspended for three matches. The press unanimously believed that the chaos could result in Barça being kicked out of *La Liga*. Meanwhile, the club continued its political journey by supporting demands to restore Catalan institutions and the statute of Catalan autonomy.

THE ARRIVAL OF DEMOCRACY

New president Josep Lluís Núñez, who stayed in power for 22 years, knew that his first duty would be to restructure the club's finances, which is why he put an end to big-money signings. This decision clearly had an impact on the sporting side, so much so that over the first few months there were already some inside the Camp Nou asking for the president's resignation. Indeed, the team had only a very minor role to play in the title race, finishing fifth that season

Many of the detractors were silenced by Barça's first Cup Winners' Cup victory, against Fortuna Düsseldorf. The match lived long in the memory:

30,000 supporters made the journey to Basle to support their team and see a 4–3 victory after extra time. The transportation of so many fans was carried out on a scale never previously seen: four special trains, 330 coaches and various charter flights, as well as coaches organized by numerous fan groups, plus private vehicles. The club helped with costs so that the price of the final was affordable for the fans, and the stands became a sea of *Azulgrana* flags and *Señeras*.

The first decade with Núñez as president, although inconsistent, allowed the team to bring home some important titles: one league title, two Cup Winners' Cups and three *Copas del Rey,* alongside some other minor honours. The standout signing in this period was Austrian Hans Krankl, who made up the permitted foreign contingent alongside Neeskens until just before the end of the 1978–79 campaign, when some negative reports about the Dutchman's private life led to him being sold, to the fans' disgust. His replacement was Dane Allan Simonsen, the 1977 *Ballon d'Or* winner. But who was managing the team itself was less clear – there were eight coaches on the bench during this decade, Kubala included. Only three of them managed to complete a whole season in the post.

Off the pitch, Núñez raised the funds required to rebuild the Camp Nou in preparation for the 1982 World Cup, held in Spain. Núñez knew how to negotiate television broadcast rights and players' image rights contracts like nobody else. It seems he had no rival when it came to numbers, which may be why the members did not ask for his resignation despite the mixed results on the pitch.

March 7, 1979, against Ipswich Town, was the last time that Barça played in their white second strip. FC Barcelona had chosen white to distinguish themselves from their dark-shirted opponents back in the Gamper days. Those white

GIJON 0
CELONA 0
CERVESA VOLL-DAMM
PRIMERA PART
CERVEZA VOLL-DAM

ABOVE: Sporting de Gijón give Barcelona a guard of honour after the *Azulgranas* sealed the title with four games to spare on March 30, 1985, having topped the table all season long.

shirts are now collectors' items. In October that year, La Masía was inaugurated as the residence for players in the youth ranks coming from outside Barcelona. It is a place that over time would become a global reference point for both the personal and sporting education of first-team players and which is now legendary. Meanwhile, member numbers kept growing, reaching 108,000 by 1986. The same growth took place in the number of supporters' clubs, which became international in their scope.

But on the pitch, the 1980s started rockily. For 1980–81, three players were signed: defender Alexanco; Asturian forward Quini, who was kidnapped for 25 days in 1981; and German Bernd Schuster, at the time the most talented central midfielder in European football. Quini's kidnapping kept his team-mates and Barça supporters on

edge, yet the team had to continue playing with morale at a low and without their top goalscorer. Unsurprisingly, the club did not end up making a title challenge and finished fifth.

To make things worse for the team, during the following season, Schuster was on the end of an aggressive tackle by Bilbao defender Andoni Goikoetxea, leaving him with a serious knee injury that kept him out of action for months. Barça went out of the *Copa* and failed to win a league that they had dominated before faltering near the end. But a second Cup Winners' Cup final victory at the Camp Nou against Standard Liège saved their season, and in June 1982, news soon broke of the signing of Argentinian Diego Maradona, who was already the best player in the world. His stint at Barcelona was brief, however, hardly two seasons in total, during which he first suffered from hepatitis and then had to overcome a serious ankle injury caused by a bad tackle, again by Goikoetxea.

The Camp Nou also experienced a historic non-sporting event before the turn of the year: for the first time, the Pope celebrated mass on Catalan territory. On a visit to Spain, John Paul II held mass in the Barça stadium, which hosted 120,000 people, a record thanks to the expansion carried out for the World Cup held a few months before.

The following 1982–83 season saw three different coaches spend time at the helm, including German Udo Lattek, who found it difficult to work with the team's two international stars. He was fired, paving the way for César Luis Menotti. Barça's title bid was unsuccessful, but a *Copa del Rey* and a less prestigious *Copa de la Liga,* both won in finals against Real Madrid, were added to the trophy cabinet.

By the end of the 1983–84 campaign, the supporters felt that something was missing. The team had two of the world's best players, although they were injured, a good squad and a World Cup-winning coach – and all they had to show for it was a Spanish *Supercopa* and a brawl in the *Copa del Rey* final against Athletic Bilbao in what would be Maradona's final match for Barça.

So in came Terry Venables, who arrived with an excellent reputation after his stints at Crystal Palace and QPR. He installed the English 4–4–2 that worked with the talented MIgueli and Julio Alberto at the back, and a midfield with Bernd Schuster, later on joined by Gary Lineker and Mark Hughes. The English coach was three years at the helm and in his first season, 1984–85, he got his hands on the *La Liga* title, their first since 1974, delighting *Los culés,* but the team would then enter a dark three-year period.

The following season would see Barça come second in all five competitions in which they competed. The recurring theme was problems related to player bonuses, contracts and the conflict between the club and one of its stars, Schuster. The German wanted to be able to negotiate his future freely, but Núñez declared that Schuster would never wear the *Azulgrana* shirt again after his apathetic performance in the European Cup final against Steaua Bucharest, a surprising defeat on the highest of stages – a final they had reached after 25 years, following a dramatic semi-final against IFK Göteborg, and which they then lost on penalties. A wounded Schuster left the stadium straight after being substituted, before the end of the match.

Núñez's opponents started to voice their opinions through the *Grupo de Opinión Barcelonista*. Barça kept on not winning, despite the signing of Gary Lineker, and finished sixth in the league that year, something which had not happened since 1965, even though they did win the *Copa del Rey,* which guaranteed them European football for the following season. The increasingly small Camp Nou crowd kept getting their white handkerchiefs out as a sign of protest against the team's play.

As if those problems were not enough, the players (with the exception of Schuster and Lineker), along with coach Luis Aragonés, summoned the press to Hotel Hesperia in order to read out a statement against the president. The *motín del Hesperia* ("Hesperia mutiny") saw the squad denounce the club for refusing to take on taxes and fines from the tax office. There were huge differences between the players and the board, including disagreements over image rights, and this impacted performances on the pitch. Financial interests were seemingly more important than playing to win. But everything changed in the space of a week when Johan Cruyff signed a contract to bring him back to FC Barcelona as coach, on May 4, 1988.

"Barcelona is more than just a football club; it's a very deeply rooted spirit that we find within ourselves, above all we value the colours."
Narcis de Carreras's presidential speech

BELOW: On November 23, 1960 Barça defeated Real Madrid 2–1 in the second leg of the last 16 of the European Cup, knocking them out. In a match riddled with controversy, English referee Reg Leafe ruled out three Real Madrid goals: one for a foul in the build-up and two were supposedly offside. Barça reached the final alongside Benfica.

RIGHT: On May 31, 1961 Barça and Benfica met at the Wankdorf Stadium in Bern, with Benfica running out 3–2 winners. The Catalan side was unlucky to hit the woodwork on four occasions and score an own goal. Incidentally the frame of the goal was changed from square-shaped to cylindrical after that match. The *culés* remember that final as "the curse of Bern".

ABOVE: Although FC Barcelona had had their eye on Johan Cruyff (left) since 1970, he was unable to join the club until the change in regulation regarding foreign signings. The Dutchman, who had already won three European Cups with Ajax, made his debut against Granada on October 28, 1973 in a 4–0 victory, netting a brace in the process.

RIGHT: The Number 9 opened his *Azulgrana* account with a tremendous strike past Izcoa five minutes into the second half, while his second was a left-footed finish into the top corner. Although Barça started the campaign in the lower reaches of the table, that match triggered a change in fortune. The Cruyff era had just begun.

TOP: *La Liga* Champions 1973–74. Back row from left to right: Sadurní, Rifé, Torres, Rinus Michels (coach), Costas, De la Cruz and Juan Carlos. Front: Rexach, Asensi, Cruyff, Sotil and Marcial.

LEFT and BELOW: A 4–2 victory at Sporting de Gijón on April 7, 1974 sealed the title for Barça with five games remaining. To the left you can see Cruyff on the coach, surrounded by hundreds of fans (below) who came to welcome back the team at Barcelona El Prat airport. They were celebrating a title that had escaped them since 1960, and would have to wait 11 years until the next one. That unforgettable season for *Los culés* included the 0–5 at the Bernabéu.

ABOVE and RIGHT: On February 17, 1974, Michels's FC Barcelona achieved something that all *culé* supporters still remember today. The five goals that Barça put past Real Madrid at the Bernabéu were the cherry on the cake in a season that was capped with a title-clinching performance in Gijón with games to spare. Cruyff, Juan Carlos and Sotil each scored once goal and Asensi twice in a *Clásico* that many saw as much more than a sporting victory because it signalled an encouraging change of cycle.

The spectators at the Bernabéu sportingly applauded the *Azulgranas* when the match came to an end. See Cruyff in action on the left and Carles Rexach on the right. "The fans were able to witness the splendid concert by the *Azulgrana* orchestra at the Bernabéu, one of the most beautiful and elegant performances in the club's illustrious history." *ABC*, February 19, 1974.

501 QUE CALORCILLO

REAL MADRID   0
BARCELONA   5

ASENSI 2 - CRUYFF-
J.CARLOS-SOTIL-

LEFT: On May 16, 1979, Joaquim Rifé's Barça won their first Cup Winners' Cup. An unprecedented 30,000 supporters made the journey to the Swiss city of Basle to witness a thrilling final against Fortuna Düsseldorf. It was all square after 90 minutes (Sánchez and Asensi scored for the *Azulgranas*) but extra-time goals by Rexach and Krankl decided the match in FC Barcelona's favour 4–3.

ABOVE: The players were welcomed home like heroes, making people forget the far from spectacular fifth-place finish in *La Liga*.

ABOVE: In 1981 Quini was kidnapped at gunpoint and held hostage in a garage in Zaragoza for 25 days. The kidnappers' inexperience facilitated his release. Barça failed to win *La Liga* that season, but did win the *Copa del Rey*. Quini was the *Pichichi* with 20 goals in 30 outings. The photo shows the day of his release on March 26, 1981.

LEFT: Johan Neeskens spent five seasons with the *Azulgranas* from 1974 to 1979. The photo shows him in action against Ipswich Town in the 1979 Cup Winners' Cup, which was the last time that Barça wore a white second strip. Following his vital contribution to the team, Neeskens became a favourite with the Barça fans and during his his last game for the club – the 4–3 victory over Fortuna Düsseldorf in the 1979 Cup Winners' Cup final – they expressed their desire for him to stay.

RIGHT: On May 12, 1982, Udo Lattek's FC Barcelona won their second Cup Winners' Cup against Standard Liège with the added incentive of playing at their home ground. The Belgians took an early lead through Vandersmissen in the seventh minute, but goals from Simonsen (44th) and Quini (63rd) completed the turn-around. The triumph saved their season as the *Azulgranas* enjoyed no domestic success, losing *La Liga* in the final few games.

JOHAN CRUYFF

To speak of Johan Cruyff (born in Amsterdam in 1947) is to speak of a footballing legend, a revolutionary figure both as a player and as a coach. FC Barcelona were immensely lucky to enjoy him in both guises, and as a player he had served under another illustrious Dutchman, Rinus Michels, who is considered by experts to be the best coach of the twentieth century. Cruyff's quality, supported by his three *Ballons d'Or* in 1971, 1973 and 1974, was demonstrated as soon as he arrived at the club. From his league debut on October 28, 1973, Barça did not lose a single match for the rest of the season and won their first *La Liga* trophy after a 14-year drought. Not only did Cruyff help win the trophy, he left his mark on the style in which it happened by playing in a way never seen before on Spanish grounds.

In his five seasons as an *Azulgrana* player, it was not just his 83 goals that made him a legend but his way of playing when he did not have the ball at his feet. Cruyff played as a centre-forward but his technique, speed and vision really made him into a "total footballer" who knew how to lose his marker and show up on the wing when nobody expected it. He was a magnificent dribbler, who not only popularized a form of gliding past players by taking advantage of a sudden change of pace from a standing position, but also gave his name to a type of dribbling: feinting as if to put in a cross or play a pass and then turning his body to touch the ball inwards with the inside of the foot – the Cruyff turn.

His assertive character led to some run-ins with referees and coaches such as Weissweiler, whose problems began as a result of substituting him in a match against Sevilla, which Barcelona ended up losing 2–0. The coach argued that Cruyff did not play well away from home and the player announced that he was leaving the club. However, the fans supported the star, and it was the coach who left his post. A few years later, his differences with the board caused him to leave the club to which he felt connected. He also named his son "Jordi", when Catalan names were still not officially permitted in Spain.

In 1988, the Dutchman became Barça coach and provided the *culé* faithful with some of their greatest moments, thanks to the "Dream Team", the first European Cup win, another five-star performance against Real Madrid, and various league titles. There was only one campaign, his last, in which the team won nothing, and after that he left the bench, conscious that an an era had ended.

"Football is a game you play with your brain. You must be in the right place, at the right time, not too early, not too late."

Johan Cruyff

DIEGO ARMANDO MARADONA

Born in 1960, Maradona arrived at FC Barcelona for a then world-record fee of 5m pounds in 1982 (7m euros). Nicknamed the *Pelusa* (Fluff), he was considered the best player in the world and one of the all-time greats. He was unable to reach the heights his talent deserved, however: firstly illness and later injuries prevented him from doing so. But there were still glorious moments, such as the memorable chip against Red Star Belgrade in the 1983 Cup Winners' Cup second round; and the goal against Real Madrid at the Bernabéu in the first leg of the *Copa de la Liga* final that same year, dribbling past the goalkeeper and a defender to score a goal that even drew applause from the home supporters.

He made his Barcelona debut on September 4, but 13 league games and six goals later he fell ill with hepatitis, which forced him to rest completely for three months. He returned with barely seven games remaining before the end of a league season that saw Barcelona finish fourth.

The following campaign was worse. On September 24, 1983, Barcelona faced reigning champions Athletic Bilbao in the league. Barça won the contest 4–0, but lost their best attacker because of a terrible tackle by defender Andoni Goikoetxea. Mardona suffered a broken ankle and damaged ligaments. A six-month recovery period was predicted following the operation, but that was almost halved and the Number 10 returned on January 8, with a brace of goals in a victory against Sevilla.

Although the team did not enjoy league success that year, they enjoyed a good run in the *Copa del Rey*, a competition that saw

Maradona's final performance in the *Azulgrana* shirt. He was sent off in the semi-finals, which banned him from the final in theory, but the Football Federation rescinded the ban and the Argentinian arrived at the match against Goikoetxea's Athletic Bilbao with feelings running high. Statements in the days leading up to the game had already added heat to a traditionally tense fixture, but the worst was yet to come.

To the astonishment of fans a Basque victory led to a pitch battle between the two teams. Maradona, among others, was suspended from Spanish competitions for three months. The *Pelusa*, hurt by the club's attitude towards the sanction, and fed up with what he considered to be refereeing injustices, put pressure on President Núñez to sell him to Napoli. The *Azulgrana* president thought it was time for him to move on, before his chaotic party lifestyle impacted on his game.

> *"If I die, I want to be reborn as myself. I'm a player who has made people happy and that's more than enough for me."*
> **Diego Armando Maradona**

4. 1988–1995: CRUYFF RETURNS AS COACH

PREVIOUS PAGES:
Ronald Koeman leads the celebratory charge after scoring an extra-time free kick in the 1992 European Cup final. The victory over Sampdoria heralded the start of a new era of success for FC Barcelona.

LEFT: Johan Cruyff's arrival as coach changed the history of Barcelona. Not only did he instil a style and way of understanding the game, but he ended the sense of victimization that restricted the club from realizing its potential. Here he is during the Cup Winners' Cup final in which Barcelona defeated Sampdoria 2–0 on May 10, 1989.

"I know the club and don't want history to repeat itself. If we want to change things, history must be changed." And so Cruyff arrived in 1988, determined to shake things up.

Over the previous few years, the club's sporting standards had fallen too low for an outfit of its stature, with 1987–88 being one of the worst seasons. Their great rivals, Real Madrid, had just won a third successive league title playing attractive football with mainly home-grown players. This Madrid team was the generation known as *la quinta del buitre* ("the vulture's cohort"), playing on the name of one of the players, Emilio Butragueño (*buitre* means "vulture" in Spanish). Meanwhile, at Barcelona, the club kept citing bad luck and woeful refereeing performances for its lack of trophies, and the players rebelled against the board for financial reasons.

Cruyff obviously knew FC Barcelona from his years as a player, and although he found the club in a difficult situation when he arrived, the board knew that he was not a man who would be easily flustered, persuaded or pleased. The strong and energetic character of *El Flaco* did not take long to shine. In order to avoid possible interference and make his authority as leader evident, he demanded total control over the dressing room and immediately carried out a purge. Less than half the players were saved from the clear-out – just 12 out of 26. "Those members of the squad who have enough dignity to wear the *Azulgrana* colours will stay at the club. All the players who are with me must respect the president. If they don't like him, they can leave." And so Cruyff made his opinion clear about the protests of the players that summer.

He also made his intentions clear to the new arrivals. His challenge that year was to bring fans back to the Camp Nou, which had had too many empty seats on match days in recent times.

The supporters were in irritable form and during the squad presentation on July 22 captain José Ramon Alexanco was booed while speaking. Cruyff decided to speak instead, in order to make it clear that they needed to look forward. "I really liked the fact that you applauded the president, but it's sad that you gave a captain that I've chosen myself a hard time. If we want to have a good season, not a bad one like the last one, we need the public's help and no more incidents like this," he insisted.

Cruyff's arrival on the coaching team seemed to many like putting a bull in a china shop, but substantial changes were needed at the club, which was about to reach its centenary, and *El Flaco* was the one to implement them. He was faced with a challenge much bigger than simply filling the Camp Nou. He also had to create a recognizable style of play, a school of football – a goal that was much more important to him than immediately winning titles. It would not be simple, and there were soon complaints about how the new arrival was imposing his famous 3–4–3 formation, even in the junior teams. The Dutchman, though, was very clear that all the club's teams had to follow the same pattern of play, one to which they would become accustomed until it formed part of their DNA, so that players who broke into the first team would be able to fit in straight away.

His old team-mate Carles Rexach joined him from the beginning. The total restructuring of the technical set-up designed by Cruyff would end up costing Barcelona 200m pesetas (1m euros) yearly. He was the best-paid coach in Europe at the time, and he arrived determined to do what he enjoyed the most: making decisions, as he himself confirmed on various occasions. He was also there to rip out the victim mentality that seemed to have taken root in the Barça psyche over previous years,

> *"I know the club and don't want history to repeat itself. If we want to change things, history must be changed."*
> **Johan Cruyff**

and to build a team that would be recognized by its movement on the pitch and become a benchmark. And he managed it. Not at the first time of asking, but he did manage it.

However, those years in which he acted with resolve, strength and creativity, immune to criticism and poor results, were not as harmonious as they have been made out to be in hindsight. Cruyff was an awkward man, and not everyone believed in him at the beginning, while he had disagreements with board members, youth-team coaches, players, journalists and the president himself. Introducing his model made him unpopular, but maybe that is where his greatness lay, in knowing how to put the club that hired him first so that it could come out of stagnation, irrespective of how his own image appeared to others.

Not only did he take charge of establishing order in the squad, but he was prepared to follow the basics of Rinus Michels's "total football", imbuing the team with his own style: open up the pitch, ask all the players to be brave and to go for one-on-ones, to demonstrate that this was an adventurous, attacking team. He planted and nurtured this seed that since then, sometimes for better, sometimes for worse, has grown to define FC Barcelona.

1988–89: CRUYFFISMO
Few players survived Cruyff's first clear-out: goalkeeper Andoni Zubizarreta, the eternal Migueli, Alexanco, Julio Alberto, Francisco Carrasco, Gary Lineker, Robert Fernández and Urbano Ortega were among the most prominent ones to stay. To complete the squad, he turned to some youth-team players who would become indispensable, such as Guillermo Amor and Luis Milla, and added international signings José Bakero, Txiki Begiristain, Andoni Goikoetxea, Julio Salinas and Eusebio Sacristán.

The season began with setbacks in the form of injuries to Bakero and Migueli, but in the eyes of the press and supporters there was no doubt that something had changed in the team's play – their historical inferiority complex and laziness had been shaken off. Cruyff managed to get the *culé* supporters excited once again in every match. Barça's attacking play that season created 80 goals – something which had not occurred since 1962 – and it shared the honour of being the team with the league's tightest defence, along with Valencia.

Of course, in the early weeks not even the players themselves were confident that things would go well. There was too much space on the pitch to defend with just three players, and they did not understand the changes imposed by the Dutchman, who sent centre-forwards such as Julio Salinas and Lineker out wide. Cruyff wanted the emphasis to be on quick touches, control and pass, and lots of rhythm, which they practised extensively using the famous *rondo* (a piggy-in-the-middle-style drill, also known as *toros* in the football world). The ball became the focal point and demanded the entire spotlight. The individual players no longer existed, the ball was the star, and the team was a whole, supportive outfit that had to work like clockwork. It's a style that is praised, applied and copied nowadays, but back then not everybody believed in it or even understood it. These were two difficult years in which Cruyff's job hung by a thread on more than one occasion.

The first time he was put under pressure was in September, just after he had arrived. The team lost 2–0 to Real Madrid in the first leg of the *Supercopa,* following three straight victories and a draw in the league. The Dutchman insisted on his 3–4–3 formation, to which his players were gradually becoming accustomed, and everything

LEFT: Ronald Koeman signed for FC Barcelona in the summer of 1989. His leadership and ability to play from deep would go on to be key in the Cruyff era.

was running smoothly until Real's first goal. Barça then fell to pieces, or rather could not string two passes together, and lost the tournament in spite of a 2–1 win in the return leg. The team lost, but in the end their style had impressed.

There was another dip in confidence after the Cup Winners' Cup round of 16 against Lech Poznań, which ended 1–1, with whistles coming from the stands, as the fans did not understand why players were out of position. Matters came to a head after elimination from the *Copa del Rey* at the hands of Atlético de Madrid, who put four goals past Barcelona despite the distinctly defensive side which Cruyff fielded on that occasion. The coach was visibly annoyed in the press conference, which saw an increase in the number of critics of his technical management. *El Flaco* ended up asking the fans for help in the form of greater support and encouragement for the team, who missed out on the league by five points. There remained only one lifeline, the Cup Winners' Cup, where both Cruyff's post and, more importantly, prestige were on the line.

On April 1, 1989, Josep Lluís Núñez was re-elected as president for a further four years, with more than 25,000 votes, while the *clásico* ended goalless at the Camp Nou. Three days later came the first leg of the Cup Winners' Cup semi-final. Barça comfortably beat CSKA Sofia 4–2, but the two goals conceded would be remembered because they were scored by a Number 8 with an explosive left foot called Hristo Stoichkov. FC Barcelona reached the final in Bern, the site of the

European Cup final defeat in 1961. But this time it was different and the match against Sampdoria, using the prescribed 3–4–3, was decided by goals from Salinas and López Recarte. So Barça got their hands on the Cup Winners' Cup.

It was not a bad note on which to end the first season of a project that had just begun and was still in its early stages, although it would be on the verge of fading away on various occasions the following year.

1989–90: A BLOCKBUSTER IN THE MAKING

Cruyff had saved the day and the season, which culminated in Lineker being shown the door, along with Romerito, a Uruguayan whom Cruyff had insisted on signing yet who did not produce the goods on the pitch. There were two new signings: Ronald Koeman and Michael Laudrup. Koeman's job was to take charge of the defence, just as he had done in the Dutch national side, which had won Euro 1988, and the PSV team, which had won the 1988 European Cup. Laudrup was expected to provide penetrating through-balls between defenders to complement the quick passing style that was being drilled into the team.

Yet from the start of the season, the style implemented by Cruyff was criticized, after the team lost to Valladolid, Oviedo and Mallorca and drew with Legia Warsaw. The match that lives longest in the memory, because of its emotional implications, was the contest on home soil against Sevilla FC before the end of the year. Barça were playing well and raced into a 3–1

RIGHT: Josep Guardiola became both a club idol and a symbol of the progress that was being made. He left his family home at a young age and even admitted to crying on numerous occasions as he went up through the ranks at La Masía. Guardiola would go on to become Barcelona captain.

lead, which was cut when the referee awarded Sevilla a debatable penalty. The team collapsed and ended up losing 4–3.

Much was said. Some players stated that the squad was lacking in confidence, the press commented on the coach without really knowing exactly what he wanted from his players, and the Dutchman added fuel to the fire by declaring that "there are many quality players, but few who also have the character and temperament required to take on responsibility" on the pitch. Cruyff missed having home-grown players who had come up through the ranks and knew how to cope with the pressure of belonging to the club. The coach had few chances left to earn a reprieve, and the only reason he was saved from dismissal in early September was because Núñez did not want to take responsibility for it, preferring to wait for the press and club members to call for Cruyff's head.

December saw defender Migueli retire after 16 years at the club. The Ceuta-born Barcelona legend is second only to Xavi in total appearances. In his testimonial game, he played alongside his old team-mates and coaches, Rexach and Cruyff.

Before the end of the year, FC Barcelona found themselves out of the Cup Winners' Cup and the European Super Cup, while they did not get higher than fourth in the league. Refereeing mistakes were blamed once again, but the excuses did not hide the team's faults. In late January, it was discovered that the club's former sporting director, Ramón Martínez, had given the president as many

as four reports belittling the system employed by the coach and attaching part of the blame for the poor results to his personality.

This was not an isolated incident. The squad also berated the coach, who made threats to players who, in his opinion, were not performing. Instead of easing off, the Dutchman reiterated his stance and stated that "you need to fight to be in the team". Given the circumstances, the supporters were also divided into two factions: those who were drawn to, and fascinated by, Cruyff's charisma and personality, as well as the change in the style of play; and those who branded him a loopy, egotistical visionary.

President Núñez was the proverbial bridge over troubled waters and the only board member to defend the coach and say that tactical mistakes were not damaging the team as much as the players' overly relaxed mindset. To top it all, Cruyff stated that he was "running out of patience" with none other than Laudrup, one of the stars of the team.

On the pitch, after overcoming Athletic Bilbao, Real Sociedad and Valencia, everyone eagerly awaited the *Copa del Rey* final, which was played on April 5, against league leaders Real Madrid. Cruyff's job seemed to depend on winning the Cup. His team won 2–0. Cruyff survived and was awarded a contract extension.

The season had not yet come to a close when newspaper *El País* published an article about the Spanish youth league which reflected the poor state of Spanish clubs' youth teams in general, something from which Barcelona were not exempt. La Masía was not yet the footballing academy it would later become when Cruyff's long-term plan – which followed in the footsteps of important youth football figures such as Jaume Olivé, Oriol Tort and Laureano Ruiz – started to produce the expected results. Just as with the first team, things were progressing slightly slower than the *Barcelonistas* would have wanted.

1990–91: THE FIRST OF FOUR LEAGUE CHAMPIONSHIP TITLES

Real Madrid had lost the previous *Copa del Rey* final, and after five years in pole position and playing scintillating football, the club seemed to be coming to the end of a cycle. Madrid captain Chendo made some unfortunate statements in which he declared that Barça did not deserve the title, as "they are not Spanish", and complained about the refereeing. Although he later qualified his words, he brought the non-sporting rivalry between the clubs back to the fore. Or maybe it was a way of expressing his frustration over the coming shift in power.

In the new season, players were incorporated into the Barça team who would not only become indispensable, but would also create their own school of football. A young Josep "Pep" Guardiola broke through from the B team, although he would play only four times that season; youth-team player Albert Ferrer was recalled from his loan spell at Tenerife; Jon Andoni Goikoetxea was brought in from Real Sociedad; and Bulgarian forward Stoichkov arrived with the European Golden Boot under his belt, after his 38-goal season. The only negative note was the mid-season exit of midfielder Luis Milla, Cruyff's first Number 4. The player had featured for the national team the season before and Real Madrid offered him more than Cruyff had wanted to pay to renew his contract.

Things were very different that year, and Barça seemed unstoppable on their path to success. They were the only team to remain undefeated in pre-season, and six straight league wins saw them shoot to the top of the league, where they would remain from Matchday Two onwards, at a comfortable distance from second-placed Real Madrid and third-placed Atlético.

This was the result of a more serious, pragmatic, effective and versatile team with a stronger core, in which defence and attack were equally important. After two years of learning how to play together, they won the title that year and put on a show doing it. Cruyff's project had finally received unanimous backing. The strategy worked perfectly with the new squad. Koeman masterfully led the rearguard, controlling the ball at the back. The midfielders played the transitional passes that were necessary for Bakero, Begiristain and Stoichkov to perform in the final third without the need for a classic Number 9. Cruyff had reinvented Barça's play, and beyond that, he had laid the foundations for the team to find its own style and achieve whatever they aimed for. He said, "That is my idea, and that is how I will present it to whoever is elected onto the board on 1 April, and if they don't like it, I'll tell them to look for another coach." That year Cruyff could afford to be more relaxed – his football was entertaining and he was winning.

The new style was closely linked to patient build-up play that didn't let the ball stop moving. The constant possession made opponents lose hope by fruitlessly chasing the ball and gradually wearing themselves out. If this seems familiar, that's because it is. This is the Barcelona style that reached another peak under Guardiola, but back then it was something new – so new that people had to get used to it. They also had to get used to winning four consecutive *La Liga* titles, for example, when only six had been clinched in the previous 40 years. Furthermore, that first league title opened the doors to a campaign in the European Cup, a trophy that had still escaped the *Azulgranas*.

But, of course, the season was not that simple. There were also problems, though the

> *"Success has no secrets; you simply must have faith in yourself, in your ideas. We have marked out our own path, drawn the line and we haven't strayed from it for even a moment."*
> **Johan Cruyff**

team overcame them maturely without blaming misfortune or victimization. There were many difficult moments. Koeman suffered a serious Achilles tendon injury, which kept him out of action from October to March. The Dutchman was effortlessly replaced by Alexanco, and he would not return until the second leg of the Cup Winners' Cup quarter-final. Stoichkov was suspended for just over two months after stamping on the referee, who had sent off Cruyff for dissent in the first leg of the *Supercopa* against Real Madrid. Both legs were lost convincingly 4–1.

The most distressing moment, however, was the emergency medical attention needed for Cruyff's heart problems after a match in Valladolid. After that, the Dutchman even starred in an anti-smoking campaign by the *Generalitat de Catalunya* (regional government of Catalonia) because his 20-a-day habit was the principal cause of his ill-health. From then on, he was seen sucking on Chupa Chups lollipops rather than his ever-present cigarettes.

During Cruyff's absence (he needed heart bypass surgery), Carles Rexach took over the reins and the team continued as normal without their first-team coach. Rexach explained in an interview how Cruyff and he complemented each other perfectly, with Rexach providing the diplomacy that the Dutchman lacked. Whatever the case, the ex-*Azulgrana* player led the team to several comfortable victories in the games in which he was in charge, including a six-goal rout of Athletic Bilbao, and a couple of draws.

But luck was not on their side in the Cup Winners' Cup final against a Manchester United side that had been under Sir Alex Ferguson's management for five years and which had just returned to European competition after the ban imposed on all English teams after the 1985 Heysel Stadium disaster. Barça conceded two goals and returned home empty-handed. However, *La Liga*

had already been wrapped up four days earlier, with four matches left to play, although a Cádiz side just one point above the relegation zone managed to annihilate Barça, 4–0. The remaining fixtures were a mere formality and Barcelona reacted by losing two and drawing one, which mattered very little. They were finally *La Liga* champions, a huge ten points clear at the top.

If anything tarnished the season, it was the murder of a young Frenchman, Frédéric Rouquier, by the *boixos nois* group, the most radical Barça followers, who also stabbed a young boy, referred to in the press only as J.M.A.M. in order to protect his identity. The reason for the attacks? Both were Espanyol fans. Rouquier's was the first violent death in Spanish football, and it shook the country, which had seen how these groups were acting without getting punished, inside and outside stadiums, for some time. In those years, skirmishes and fights between Barça, Espanyol, Real Madrid and Atlético fans were commonplace. Most of the participants were skinheads whose far-right ideology used football as a conduit for their violent, and often criminal, activities.

FC Barcelona denied that they financed the *boixos nois*, but it is true that the group enjoyed certain privileges at the ground. The father of one of the members arrested over the murder even accused the club, and specifically vice-president Joan Gaspart, of encouraging and tolerating violence, as his son, like the rest of the *boixos*, got free entry into the Camp Nou without a ticket or membership card. The constant liveliness, noise and colour these groups brought to the terraces was the argument used by clubs for allowing them access to their grounds and making it easier for them to obtain tickets and travel to other stadiums.

This is perhaps the darkest and most neglected chapter in the history of a club that wanted to stand

for respect, tolerance and solidarity. Yet, more than 20 years would go by before effective steps were taken, under Laporta, to stamp out this scourge.

1991–92: THE TREBLE: LA LIGA, SUPERCOPA AND THE FIRST EUROPEAN CUP

With the league trophy in their grasp, there was a positive start to the new season, although the team needed to show that FC Barcelona's attractive, creative and effective football was not a mere one-off. Maybe that is why, at the beginning of the campaign, Cruyff sent out a message calling for a renewed effort: "If you want to be successful, you have to sweat blood." This was the year they had to do it all again – to give their all and then some – in order to claim the title that had always escaped the almost 100-year-old club: the European Cup. But it should not be forgotten that the coach's main aspiration was to retain the league title, something it had not managed since 1960.

The start of Barça's title defence was more than erratic: the team lost four out of the first seven matches and did not reach third in the table until Matchday 14. But three games later, Barça were second. Just as the Dutch coach had said in a report given to management about the previous season, "Success has no secrets; you simply must have faith in yourself, in your ideas. We have marked out our own path, drawn the line and we haven't strayed from it for even a moment."

And so, whether the team won or lost, Cruyff decided to remain faithful to a philosophy in which he believed totally, and which so many other

coaches would subsequently copy. He made hardly any changes to the squad, and very few new signings, although the increasing presence of a home-grown midfielder, who had made his first-team debut against Cádiz in December 1990, was becoming significant. Josep Guardiola was gifted with great vision and incredible passing precision. Over time he acquired the role of being the anchor of the team, the conductor of their play, a model that future generations of midfielders would follow.

Barcelona remained in second place until the last moment, and on the last day of the season they defeated Athletic Bilbao 2–0 to set up a grandstand finale. That afternoon the fans' attention was drawn to Tenerife, where Real Madrid, league leaders all season, were playing for the title. Tenerife, with Jorge Valdano as coach, were losing 2–1, but an own goal by Real defender Rocha followed by a Tenerife goal one minute later gave them a famous victory and Barcelona the league. Barça had scraped it by just one point, and at the last minute – but as directors, coaches and players like to remind everybody, that's football.

This was not the only triumph: the *Supercopa* was won in October against Atlético de Madrid, and the European Cup had been clinched just 18 days before *La Liga*. Getting to the final in Wembley was far from simple and the supporters still remembered the epic second leg against Kaiserslautern in the second round. Barcelona had a two-goal advantage from the first leg but the German side scored three times at home. Ten seconds remained until the end and elimination,

ABOVE: In the 1991–92 season Barcelona won La Liga and the European Cup, in the process developing the confidence necessary to put paid to the ghosts of the past.

RIGHT: Hristo Stoichkov is tackled by Moreno Mannini during the European Cup final on May 20, 1992, at Wembley. Sampdoria had a great team that included the likes of Gianluca Pagliuca, Roberto Mancini, Gianluca Vialli and Toninho Cerezo.

when an imposing Bakero header kept Barça in the competition.

The final, against Sampdoria from Genoa, was no less exciting, as extra time arrived with the score 0–0. Koeman broke the deadlock with a free kick in the 111th minute in front of the 25,000 *culé* supporters who had gone to London to experience an historic moment. After 93 years, on May 20, 1992, Barça won their first European Cup. Cruyff's advice to his players, before they went out on the pitch, was: "It is not worth suffering so much to get this far and still be scared of losing. Let out a smile, go out there and enjoy yourselves in this beautiful stadium. Playing in a final in the birthplace of football is priceless."

The "Dream Team" was enjoying its sweetest moment. Criticism and comments about the team's defensive vulnerability were put to one side. As were the rows that the Dutchman had with Stoichkov – the coach substituted him on various occasions and the Bulgarian was not the type to take such decisions well – and also with president Núñez, who was rumoured to be hardly speaking to the coach. Even the feeling that the *Copa del Rey* had slipped through their grasp on penalties against Valencia in the last 16 of the competition was forgotten – for a while.

Other issues were postponed but not forgotten, such as the far from quiet struggle for sporting and administrative control – over signings, bonuses, contract renewals and so on – between the coach and the board of directors, in which there was no shortage of strong words exchanged.

Meanwhile, *La Generalitat* awarded the team the *Creu de Sant Jordi I* (a civil distinction awarded to those who help promote Catalonia's global image) and the fans filled the streets – the newspapers claimed a million people – to celebrate the success of a team that still did not know it would soon become legendary. That summer, Barcelona also had the honour of hosting the Olympic Games, and the party continued.

1992–93: ANOTHER TREBLE
The same non-sporting issues as in the previous season were at the forefront once again as the post-treble and Olympic hangover lingered. Stoichkov, whose peculiar personality gripped the Barcelona supporters, still kept his fractured relationship with the coach alive. Cruyff himself continued his crusade against the board, from whom he demanded greater control of the dressing room. Núñez refused but offered the coach a new contract, which was rejected again and again. January arrived and after the president agreed to some of the Dutchman's requests, excluding the one to make him manager, Cruyff signed. Koeman, the scorer of the European Cup final goal, also signed a two-year extension that season.

On the pitch, the first league fixture was against a Real Madrid side that arrived in low spirits. Stoichkov, who superciliously joked that they would put as many goals (seven) past *Los Merengues* as they had put past CSKA Sofia in the Joan Gamper Trophy, scored the winning

> *"Enjoy yourselves in this beautiful stadium. Playing in a final in the birthplace of football is priceless."*
> **Johan Cruyff**

Barcelona goal three minutes from time, when the score was 1–1. Barça started well that season, not taking long to reach second place in the table, and conquered top spot soon after, for which they vied with the old enemy, Real Madrid. As the league campaign wore on and with Barça on cruise control, Guardiola and Goikoetxea were injured, which the ever-belligerent Cruyff blamed on their international duty with the Spanish national team, then coached by Javier Clemente.

The first trophy arrived in late October in the shape of the *Supercopa,* which pitted Barcelona against Altético de Madrid. Barça put three goals past their opponents, conceding just one on home turf. Their first test was passed, with flying colours. But the second test was failed. Barcelona were knocked out of the European Cup in the last 16. After a 1–1 draw in Moscow, CSKA arrived at the Camp Nou ready to destroy Barça's dreams of retaining the trophy, and defeated the *Azulgranas* 3–2. Barça's first Intercontinental Cup entry was also unsuccessful, as Sao Paulo ran out 2–1 winners in the final in Tokyo.

On Christmas Eve, Núñez announced his plan to stand for re-election as president during a period in which many clubs were about to become public limited companies. He declared it was his intention to protect Barça from that process and instead suggested the creation of a foundation, as well as an expansion in the club's assets, by building a training complex and a student residence near the Camp Nou. In January 1993, Núñez ran unopposed and renewed his term in office for a further five years, as stipulated in the new club regulations. And so began the process by which FC Barcelona would become a foundation and not fall into the hands of unwanted investors.

As the weeks went by, some other matters were gradually settled. Guardiola extended his contract until 1995, and did so on half the salary offered by Inter and Roma, who coveted his signature. The gesture was especially appreciated by the fans, as he was a home-grown player. Stoichkov – after publicly announcing his unhappiness with the Dutch coach and hanging his future at the club on Cruyff's attitude – stopped flirting with Paris Saint-Germain and declared that he had decided to stay at Barcelona for the rest of his career. In March, goalkeeper and team captain Zubizarreta lifted the European Super Cup after beating Werder Bremen. It was the second title of the campaign.

As for *La Liga*, it was almost a re-run of the year before: Barça had been top of the table for ten weeks until May 30, when they had fallen one point behind Real Madrid. *Los Merengues* needed to beat Tenerife and Barça had to do the same against Real Sociedad. Tenerife won 2–0 and FC Barcelona clinched their third consecutive league title. That year the town hall awarded the club the city's Gold Medal for Sporting Merit.

1993–94: THE FOURTH AND FINAL TITLE
It was Cruyff's sixth season in the dugout, making him the club's longest-serving manager thanks to good results, the style of play which he had devised, a vibrant personality and the confidence which the members, board and, of course, the players contributed to the project.

The upcoming season would have a standout performer: Romário de Souza. The Brazilian arrived from PSV Eindhoven with the promise of scoring at least 30 goals per season. Just to make it clear that he was not all talk, he scored a hat trick on his league debut against Real Sociedad, the first of five that season. The beast was unleashed. His incredible dummying and monumental talent delighted the public and even opposition coaches. Jorge Valdano, who was always generous in his

> *"If it was hard living by his side, it will be much harder coping with his ghost ... Cruyff is leaving, one obstacle less en route to mediocrity."*
> **El País**

appreciation of those who demonstrated value and virtue, went as far as to brand Romario a "cartoon" player, on account of his outlandish feats.

Everything was more or less going to plan, although some incomprehensible draws and defeats against lesser teams, such as Lleida and Logroñés, made the coach fine the players for their poor performances at the end of the year. Maybe as a reaction to the punishment, the squad – after losing to Real Madrid in the *Supercopa* and conceding twice to Sporting de Gijón – sealed a memorable 5–0 win over their nemesis in white. This came exactly 20 years after Barça's famous 5–0 win at the Bernabéu, in which Cruyff had played. Romário took home the match ball after a superb hat trick.

However, the *Azulgranas* were gradually knocked out of the other competitions. A surprising defeat against second-division Betis would eliminate them from the *Copa del Rey* quarter-finals. As for the Champions League, FC Barcelona were brilliantly passing all their tests, including a comeback against Dynamo Kiev, but imploded in the final in Athens, losing 4–0 to an indisputably superior AC Milan side just three days after clinching the league title in the last minute once again. *La Liga* was the only title for the "Dream Team" that year, signifying the start of the end of a cycle.

Looking back at that season, it is clear that the coach was already showing signs of impatience with the relaxed attitude of certain players, and he threatened to replace underperforming *vacas sagradas* ("sacred cows") with youth-team players. The dressing room rebelled under the pressure from their coach and went to the board, but Núñez, who had just started the Foundation, seemed to agree with the Dutchman's iron-fist approach. The points dropped in the league seemed to suggest the coach was right to show greater trust in the youth-team players, who had already been groomed in the first team's style of play.

Clinching that title made the supporters happy, although it arrived, literally, at the last instant. Barça ended up level on points with Deportivo de la Coruña, but had a favourable head-to-head record. That day Barcelona had defeated Sevilla 5–2, while the Galician team missed the opportunity to take home the title when Valencia goalkeeper, González, saved a Đukić penalty in the 89th minute.

INSPIRATION FADES

The resounding setback against AC Milan in Athens caused the already slightly fractured squad to split up. After being knocked out of the *Copa del Rey* against Betis, the players requested a meeting without the coach present in order to try to resolve their problems. Fines were still being issued to players considered by Cruyff to have let the team down by poor performances or dissent to referees. Stoichkov was one such player and was one of the most commonly sent-off team members.

The World Cup in the USA had just taken place that summer, but this didn't stop recently crowned world champion Romário from receiving his first reprimand and fine for reporting back for pre-season 23 days late. However, Cruyff was unable to make this sanction stick, and was forced to select the Brazilian for the first league game because Stoichkov and Hagi were absent. The "Dream Team" increasingly resembled a jigsaw puzzle that was gradually losing pieces, some as important as Laudrup, Julio Salinas, Zubizarreta and Goikoetxea. Over Christmas, Romário announced that he wanted to join Flamengo. Stoichkov won the *Ballon d'Or*, but his ongoing battle with Cruyff saw him leave for AC Parma at the end of the campaign. Koeman, Begiristain and Eusebio also wanted to take up fresh challenges.

LEFT: Luís Figo – the hero who would become a villain. He was one of Johan Cruyff's last signings in 1995. The Portuguese winger would go on to become club captain and the driving force of the team in the seasons to come.

Cruyff looked to the youth teams for new players, but the squad did not have the necessary depth to maintain the high standards from previous years. The season ended with a *Supercopa* victory, but only fourth place in the league. This was not good enough. Real Madrid, now with Laudrup in the squad, were champions that year and also got revenge on Barcelona for the 5–0 humiliation at the Camp Nou the season before. They were not the only ones to put five goals past Barça; Racing de Santander did the same just one month later.

Cruyff's final year at the helm was noteworthy because of the massive influx of players from the B team, with more than 20 of them appearing at some stage, as well as the signings of Luís Figo and Gica Popescu. Although it was the Dutchman's only season not to produce a trophy, performances were good and the team finished third, a commendable achievement with a squad mainly formed of young home-grown players.

The consolidation of a comprehensive, wide-ranging academy programme was another of the great legacies that Cruyff left at Barça. The Dutch coach was crucial to the development of the football academy, which he had suggested himself to Núñez in 1978, when he had already left the club as a player. La Masía turned from idea to reality one year later, in October 1979. Although Cruyff would subsequently earn some enemies by his purging of coaches who refused to follow his instructions, he knew how to get the most out of the players like nobody else, as shown by Amor, Milla, Ferrer, Guardiola and Carles Busquets.

Cruyff's relationship with the club management, to which he had given so much sucess, did not end well. On May 18, 1996, Núñez sacked Cruyff through vice-president Gaspart, two games before the end of the season and without giving him the opportunity to say goodbye to the *culé* faithful. Rexach, as ordered by the board, was in the dugout for the final home game of the season against Celta de Vigo, played the very next day. Raucous applause was heard from the terraces when Jordi Cruyff was substituted and threw his shirt into the crowd. The reception belonged to his father.

The supporters were very much on the side of the coach who had changed Barça history forever – or, at the very least, they were against the way in which he was shown the door. "That's not how to do it" read the white handkerchiefs that were waved each time the president appeared in the directors' box. An array of banners confirmed that the overwhelming majority of supporters were behind Cruyff. There was a lot of affection towards *El Flaco*, despite his sharp remarks, outbursts, contradictions and peculiar nature. "Johan, don't be long", "Johan, forgive them, because they don't know what they're doing", "Cruyff, we love you" and "Cruyff yes, Núñez no" were just some examples of the comments fans were making. "It's a bitter pill to swallow. It hurts. It's more a lack of respect to the members and people than it is to me," declared the coach in his final press conference. And so the man who had done the most to restore pride in the club's colours left, without a tribute.

Valdano excellently summarized how life would be at Barça from then on in an article published in the newspaper *El País* a few days after the coach's dismissal: "If it was hard living by his side, it will be much harder coping with his ghost." And he concluded: "Cruyff is leaving, one obstacle less en route to mediocrity."

"If you want to be successful, you have to sweat blood."
Johan Cruyff

LEFT: The starting line-up in the Cup Winners' Cup final in Switzerland on May 10, 1989, against Sampdoria. From left to right, back: Zubizarreta, Salinas, Lineker, Roberto, Aloisio, Eusebio, Alexanko; front: Txema Corbet, Amor, Urbano, Beguiristain, Milla, Angel Mur.

ABOVE: Barcelona beat Sampdoria 2–0 to claim the Cup Winners' Cup title, and Roberto holds aloft the trophy. The era of Johan Cruyff combined attractive football with victories in big games – for fans, the only history worth remembering.

ABOVE: The Barcelona players and fans celebrate beating Real Madrid 2–0 in the 1990 *Copa del Rey* final. This result may have radically changed the club's history. Barcelona came out victorious, but it has been written that if the old enemy had won, it could have constituted the end for Johan Cruyff. It was the season before the "Dream Team" era began. Goals by Guillermo Amor and Julio Salinas helped put an end to the dominance of Real Madrid and the *Quinta del Buitre*, on the back of five straight league titles.

"You need to fight to be in the team."
Johan Cruyff

LEFT and BELOW: The 1991–92 season was unforgettable. Not only did FC Barcelona win the much sought-after European Cup, but they also clinched the *Supercopa* and *La Liga* after severing Real Madrid's seemingly unassailable eight-point lead in the last few games of the campaign.

FOLLOWING PAGES: The Barcelona support at Wembley for the 1992 European Cup Final: on that day in London so much historical pressure was lifted and the feeling of victimization was left to one side. From that moment onwards the trophy cabinet would welcome regular additions in the club's most glorious period of success.

LEFT and BELOW: No Barcelona fan will forget May 20, 1992. After 90 minutes the match was all square. Ronald Koeman's extraordinary free kick in the 111th minute beat Gianluca Pagliuca and won Barça's first European Cup.

RIGHT: José Ramón Alexanco changed his kit to lift the European Cup. On the team's return home, more than one million Barcelona supporters took to the streets to celebrate. It was the day when a young Guardiola lifted the cup on the balcony at the town hall in the emblematic Sant Jaume square, to cries of *"Ja la tenim aquí"*, emulating Catalonian president Tarradellas on his return from exile after Franco's death.

LEFT: The FC Barcelona "Dream Team" was a mix of homegrown Spanish players and international imports. From left to right: Josep Guardiola, Albert Ferrer, Hristo Stoichkov, Ronald Koeman and José Maria Bakero in training in 1993. They retained *La Liga* in 1992–1993 in their third straight league success under Cruyff. One more would follow.

ABOVE: Johan Cruyff congratulates his commanding Dutch defender Ronald Koeman during celebrations following another league title in May 1993. Barcelona won the title for the third successive season, finishing a single point ahead of Real Madrid. It seemed as if the era of success would last forever. But everything must come to an end.

FOLLOWING PAGES: The 1993–94 Barcelona team celebrating their fourth and final consecutive league success.

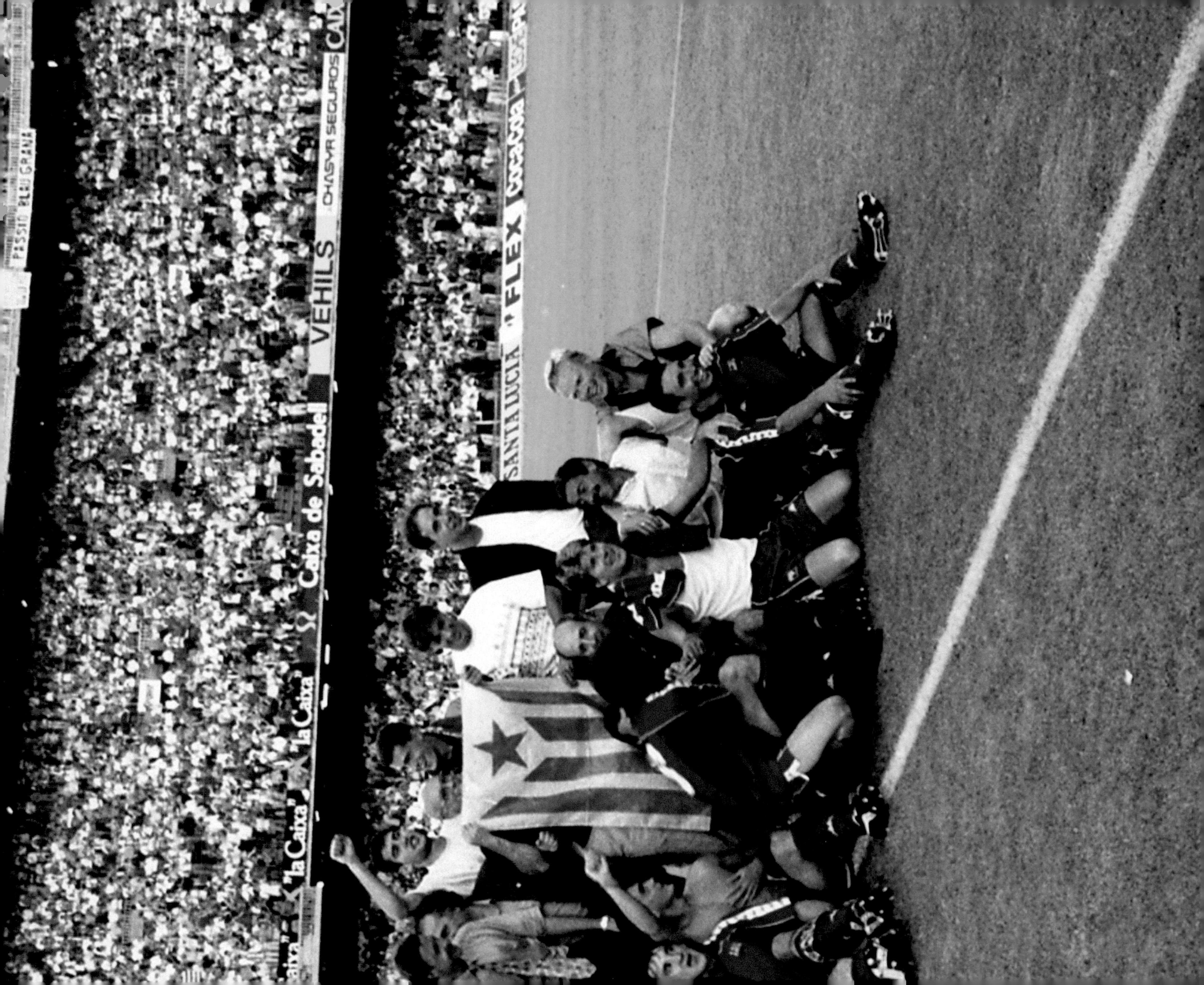
VEHILS
Caixa de Sabadell
"la Caixa"
FLEX
SANTALUCIA

"Finding out Laudrup wasn't in the starting line-up really settled my nerves. It was a mistake by Cruyff."
Fabio Capello

ABOVE: A dream fixture against AC Milan in the 1994 European Cup final soon turned into a nightmare. Daniele Massaro slots home the first of his two first-half goals in a painful 4-0 defeat that would signal the end of the Johan Cruyff era. Milan's other goals came from Dejan Savićević and Marcel Desailly.

RIGHT: Fabio Capello after AC Milan's 4-0 win in the European Cup final: "There was just one player who scared me: Michael Laudrup. Finding out he wasn't in the starting line-up really settled my nerves. It was a mistake by Cruyff."

"It hurts. It's more
a lack of respect to
the members and
people than
it is to me."
Johan Cruyff

LEFT: The confrontation between Cruyff and the board
reached breaking point on May 18, 1996. President Josep
Lluís Núñez announced the sacking of the coach with
two league games remaining. Carles Rexach was his
successor in the interim before Bobby Robson's arrival.
Protests defending the Dutchman could be heard during
the final league match at the Camp Nou.

MICHAEL LAUDRUP

Michael Laudrup (born in Frederiksberg, Denmark, in 1964) arrived at FC Barcelona in 1989, during Cruyff's second year as coach. The Dane's *Serie A* experience at Juventus had been far from impressive, possibly because his time there coincided with some of the best forwards of the era, and so many questioned the new signing's suitability. However, Cruyff's offensive tactics required someone who knew how to play in between lines of players and to drag opposition centre-backs out of position, causing them to switch off when it came to marking. He was a generous forward who knew how to be a team player and play the crucial final ball. Laudrup fitted into Cruyff's system and became one of his most creative forwards. His excellent vision not only helped him provide countless assists, but he also knew where the goal was, netting some screamers along the way. He scored 55 goals in 216 official matches as an *Azulgrana*.

The fact that he would occasionally go missing on the pitch jeopardized his Barça future from his second season onwards. However, he survived thanks to his ability to bounce back and adapt to the peculiar circumstances of a team in which collective play took precedence over big stars. He was one of the pillars of the "Dream Team", alongside Stoichkov, Koeman, Guardiola and Bakero, which knew how to selflessly exploit the talent at its disposal.

While at Barcelona, Laudrup was awarded Player of the Year in 1992 and, apart from the titles, his time spent at the Catalan team, combined with his two seasons at Real Madrid, made up his finest days as a footballer.

The Dane's spell as an *Azulgrana* was occasionally peppered with disagreements with Cruyff, who had been his childhood idol. (Laudrup even went so far as to say he could not stand him.) Years later, though, he would confess that Cruyff was the coach who taught him the most. He made the decision to leave when the coach left him out of the squad for the 1994 Champions League final against AC Milan because he could select only three foreign players. Milan's coach, Fabio Capello, would later say that Laudrup was the player he feared the most.

Laudrup played for Real Madrid the following season, and figured in the match in which *Los Merengues* put five past Barça, having been an *Azulgrana* in the 5–0 win over Madrid at the Camp Nou the year before. Sometime later he wisely reflected on one of the keys behind the success of the "Dream Team": "We played very good football, and showed that, even without having the ten best players in the world, you could have the best team."

"Pelé was the player of the 70s, Maradona of the 80s and Laudrup of the 90s."
Franz Beckenbauer

HRISTO STOICHKOV

Stoichkov was a rebellious "bad boy" but at the same time a friendly character bursting with talent. He was one of the indisputable stars in the "Dream Team", and a fans' favourite, despite – or because of – his temperamental and confrontational nature, which earned him various red cards, reprimands and bans. That fighting character shone most brightly when the Barça colours, which he made his own from the very beginning, needed to be defended seriously. Maybe it was that combative and predatory spirit that led Cruyff to sign him, after noticing his hunger for goal while playing for CSKA Sofia in the Cup Winners' Cup semi-final in April 1989. Cruyff then came

year, as he was thinking about joining Napoli. Maradona made him drop that idea, when the transfer was almost sealed. Furthermore, his ties to the team and the city were already too strong, as he confessed himself. So strong that he made a promise never to play for another Spanish team. And he kept it, which was another reason the fans loved him so much.

Yet, in spite of their differences, Stoichkov now thanks the Dutch coach for what he taught him, just as Laudrup does. In an interview conducted in 2013 with *Jot Down* magazine, he confessed that Cruyff had changed "some aspects of my game, he moved me, but the people don't understand

ROMÁRIO DA SOUZA

Romário's stay at FC Barcelona was short, but intense and eventful. It would not be possible to describe Barça's history without discussing this brilliant player. The man nicknamed the "cartoon" player by Jorge Valdano, on account of his outlandish abilities, was the finisher that the "Dream Team" needed in order to be a really breath-taking side.

Born in Rio de Janeiro, Brazil in 1966, Romário was playing for PSV Eindhoven in 1993, when Barcelona signed him on a three-year contract. He was a quick forward, whose dribbling, finishing and ability to lose his marker made him lethal. He made a promise of scoring 30 goals in his first season at Barça – and he kept it. He enjoyed an excellent season, scoring five hat tricks (one of which was against Real Madrid) and four braces. (Five hat tricks is a feat bettered only by Lionel Messi in 2011–12.)

One of his goals against *Los Merengues* was particularly memorable because of its execution. Twenty years later, the *barcelonista* press still reminisce about it. Its fame derives from a dribble that Brazilians call the "cow tail" because of its resemblance to a cow's tail flicking around to swat away flies. He started by receiving the ball with his back to goal and then made a spectacular 180-degree turn, and a vicious change of pace took him past defender Rafael Alkorta to enable him to finish coolly with a deft flick past the Madrid keeper. Romario enjoyed himself on the pitch, like any good Brazilian, and his eye for goal was complemented by the imagination with which he scored his goals.

Romário's second season at Barça was neither as festive nor as celebrated. Cruyff did not forgive him for returning from his holidays almost a month late, and although he selected him for the first league match due to a lack of alternatives, their relationship was put under strain by the player's continual trips to Brazil. The eventual breakdown with the coach caused the Brazilian to leave for Flamengo in January 1995, with his World Cup winners' medal under his belt. Although it was a premature exit, the admiration that the Barcelona fans feel towards this prodigious goalscorer has not waned. His final outing in *Azulgrana* colours took place at the Bernabéu on January 7, when *Los Merengues* got their revenge by putting five goals past Barcelona.

He was the star player at the World Cup in the USA, although Brazil left its *jogo bonito* to one side in order to adapt to a more pragmatic and effective European style of football. Romário scored five of Brazil's 11 goals. Without doubt, 1994 was his best year: *La Liga* with Barça, a World Cup with Brazil, the *Pichichi* as top scorer in *La Liga* and FIFA World Player of the Year. After his departure for Flamengo, and despite still being a truly great player who kept scoring impossible goals, his star gradually faded.

> "I feel lucky that we had Romário at Barcelona. He's a goalscorer with the heart of a champ."
> **Hristo Stoichkov**

5. 1996–2008: POST-CRUYFF, PRE-GUARDIOLA

PREVIOUS PAGES:
Barcelona enjoyed both
domestic and international
success with Frank Rijkaard
as manager and Ronaldinho
performing on the pitch.
Here, the *Azulgrana*
players celebrate Juliano
Belletti's winner in the 2006
Champions League final.

LEFT: Leo Messi's
footballing education began
in Rosario, Argentina. His
journey to Barcelona and
rise through *La Masía*
culminated in his full debut
in 2004. Between 2008
and 2013 he performed as
nobody had ever previously
done in football.

After Cruyff's rushed and poorly managed departure, *barcelonismo* had to face up to a new reality. The bad-tempered but brilliant Dutchman, the architect of an almost decade-long project, was no longer at the helm. But *El Flaco*'s legacy continued to loom over the *Azulgranas* in multiple forms, all the way down to the youth teams that played two-touch, total football in an offensive 3–4–3 system that the supporters, including those of other clubs, loved. Worse still, Cruyff remained in the city to offer his opinion on everything Barcelona-related.

There is no doubt that under Cruyff, *los culés* finally shook off the sense of resignation and victimization that surrounded the club. The *barcelonistas* were able to proudly defend not only their colours but also a style of play, just as Johan had wanted. The fans became so accustomed to this style that now they demanded nothing less. Perhaps that explains the cold welcome received by that highly competent veteran Sir Bobby Robson. The English coach did not deserve some of the ill-treatment meted out to him, such as the resounding boos he got during an 8–0 annihilation of Logroñés. Robson confessed to British journalist John Carlin just how surprised he was at the reaction: "You won't believe it, John. Here we win, we score a shed load of goals, but they don't stop criticizing me. We scored six against Rayo Vallecano the other day and the Camp Nou was whistling because they didn't think the quality of football was up to scratch! I don't understand it, I promise you."

Yes, the team won games and clinched three titles that season, but the general consensus on the terraces was: "We're not playing well." Cruyff's style was far more deeply rooted than can be imagined. *Los culés* no longer accepted simple victories; they demanded excellence and spectacular wins, in the "Dream Team" style. This

is why Robson's triumphs were not met with much joy.

There were two standout signings that year. The first was a man from Gijón, who arrived via Real Madrid, and who would become a fans' favourite – Luis Enrique. The second was the Brazilian Ronaldo. Almost half of the club's transfer fund was invested in signing Ronaldo, who was considered by many to be the best in the world at the time and who cost around 15m euros. The Brazilian's performances on the pitch showed that this was money well spent.

As a side issue, Robson arrived in Barcelona accompanied by a young helper with whom he had already worked at Sporting Lisbon and FC Porto, José Mourinho. Although Robson departed at the end of the season, Mourinho remained on the coaching staff, no longer just as an interpreter but also writing reports, and some time would pass before his contract expired in July 2000.

After the disastrous 1995–96 campaign, the one under the Englishman was not bad at all. Success arrived in the shape of a battling *Supercopa* win over Atlético de Madrid (a 5–2 win at home followed by a 3–1 loss away); a fourth Cup Winners' Cup, after a Ronaldo penalty against Paris Saint-Germain; and a *Copa del Rey* campaign that had Barça fans' hearts racing. The first leg of the quarter-finals against Atlético de Madrid ended 2–2 and the *Azulgranas* found themselves 3–0 down at half time during the return leg. An electric atmosphere inside the ground filled the team with confidence, and they pulled off an astonishing comeback to win 5–4.

The final at the Bernabéu was no less enthralling, with Betis taking the lead twice, only to end up losing to an extra-time Figo goal as the clock neared midnight. The highlight from that night has musical overtones: the Barça vice-president, Joan Gaspart, personally ensured

RIGHT: Bobby Robson took over at Barcelona following Johan Cruyff's departure. The club was divided and did not know how to incorporate Robson's alternative ideas. The Englishman lasted only one year in the post despite winning three trophies.

that the *Cant del Barça* would be played over the tannoy up to four times, to the joy and surprise of the Barcelona supporters present. Real Madrid president Lorenzo Sanz did not see the funny side. Mourinho celebrated an *Azulgrana* victory at the Bernabéu that night – and there are photos to prove it.

As well as the three titles, the International Federation of Football History and Statistics (IFFHS) proclaimed that Barcelona were the best team in the world that season and they finished second in *La Liga*, just two points behind Real Madrid. But in spite of everything, public and media opinion insisted that not enough of a show was on offer, and Robson was replaced as coach. He did remain at the club for an extra year, however, moving "upstairs" to the position of general manager.

THE VAN GAAL YEARS

The gentle-mannered Briton made way for Louis van Gaal, an outspoken, stubborn Dutchman who arrived at the club as it had just lost its biggest star, Ronaldo. Against all the odds, considering the poor performances exhibited at the beginning of the season, Barça ended up having a successful campaign.

But the best player in the world left the club. An extension agreement had seemingly been reached after an improved contract was offered, but Ronaldo's representatives unilaterally decided on his departure for Inter Milan, who agreed to pay his 24m euro release clause. One Brazilian

may have left, but two others arrived – Rivaldo and "Sonny" Anderson – as did Dutchmen Ruud Hesp and Michael Reiziger. Presidential elections were held that summer, and Núñez won at a canter, with 76 percent of the votes.

It was not a bad year: the team won its first league and cup double since 1959. If you throw in a European Super Cup victory over Borussia Dortmund, you could say the team was doing well. They were in pole position in the league from Day One, and would hardly relinquish it all season. Nine points separated them from the runners-up, Athletic Bilbao. Furthermore, there were home and away victories over a Real Madrid side that would battle for the league title before dropping away towards the close, although they ended up becoming European champions.

A penalty shoot-out was needed to defeat Mallorca in the *Copa del Rey* final after a 1–1 draw. Despite everything, the supporters were not satisfied with a team that they did not recognize as their own, nor with a coach whose communication skills left much to be desired. *Las Noticias del Guiñol*, the Spanish version of *Spitting Image*, went as far as to use a wall of bricks with hair to represent Van Gaal's face. For some reason, spirits were at a low.

In non-sporting affairs, the candidates in the club's opposition party, *Elefant Blau* (Blue Elephant), had been attempting for some time to oust Núñez, who had been president for two decades. Among other suggestions, they proposed a limit on terms in office. *Elefant*

> *"We scored six ... and the Camp Nou was whistling because they didn't think the quality of football was up to scratch!"*
> **Bobby Robson**

Blau's leader and spokesman was Joan Laporta and the group was endorsed by the influential Johan Cruyff. They managed to call a vote of no confidence, but this did not succeed and Núñez remained in his post.

1998–99: A CENTURY OF *BARCELONISMO*

Barça turned 100 years old. Although the anniversary was technically in late 1999, the board decided to dedicate a whole year of festivities to mark the occasion, the first of which took place in November 1998. Unfortunately it was not the most brilliant of seasons to mark the club's centenary. By the time the first anniversary event was held, Barça had lost in the *Supercopa* against Mallorca, a match in which a very young Xavi Hernández made his debut and scored the only *Azulgrana* goal of the tournament. As the season progressed, the team experienced more draws and defeats than victories in *La Liga* and the Champions League.

The event to open the festivities was witnessed by 100,000 spectators at the Camp Nou, who enjoyed the *Azulgrana* anthem sung by self-proclaimed *culé* Joan Manel Serrat, a huge music icon in Catalonia, Spain and Latin America in general. The club was teeming with commemorative acts, including a poster designed by painter Antoni Tàpies and a performance by tenor José Carreras.

One of the most exciting attractions was the parade by all the players who had represented FC Barcelona, the same day as a match against Brazil featuring ex-*Azulgrana* Ronaldo and ending 2–2. A street parade through the city was also scheduled. It included four buses for each of the four league titles that Barça won that year in football, basketball, handball and hockey, which reinforced the multi-sporting nature of the club. That season the team played in a kit inspired by the first one worn by Gamper and company,

with just one stripe of each colour, blue and red, adorning each side of the chest.

Autonomous Catalan television broadcast a weekly programme dedicated to the club all year round. The final piece was huge and entitled "One hundred years of *Azulgrana* passion". In April 1999, a plethora of club representatives (not including the coach, who had prior commitments) enjoyed an audience with Pope John Paul II, who was presented with a centenary gold medal. Andrés Iniesta, a youth-team player at the time, was also at the party.

To round it all off, a tribute match to Cruyff and the "Dream Team" was arranged, despite his damaged relationship with the board. It was a sell-out, in which *El Flaco* had 15 players from that era at his disposal, including Koeman, Bakero, Laudrup, Stoichkov, Salinas and Begiristain. Van Gaal's Barça were the victorious opponents, running out 2–0 winners.

But the season had not started well. As well as losing the *Supercopa*, a succession of inexplicable draws and defeats in *La Liga* left Barcelona in tenth place after 14 games, and the press and supporters started calling for Van Gaal's head. However, after such a shaky start, an equally surprising recovery saw Barça win the league, 11 points clear of second-placed Real Madrid. It seemed as if the team had been gradually absorbing the Dutchman's system, which got the fans hooked once again in the final furlong.

Everything else went wrong, however. Valencia knocked them out in the *Copa del Rey* quarter-finals, and they were unable to progress past the Champions League group stages in the year when the final would be played at the Camp Nou. Van Gaal was still unable to make many friends in the press or among Barça supporters. That mission to build some bridges became more onerous when the three Dutchmen already at

FOLLOWING PAGES:
When Barcelona decided to set a Guinness World Record by decorating the Camp Nou with the biggest flag in the world, they chose *la señera* rather than one containing the club's colours. It was displayed during the Joan Gamper Trophy on August 25, 2004.

"Friends in the press, I'm leaving. Congratulations."
Louis van Gaal

the club were joined by five more. Having eight players with the same nationality as the coach was too much for the fans' liking. It must be remembered that clubs were now able to sign as many foreigners from within the European Union as they wanted, thanks to the Bosman ruling of late 1995. This decreed that if unlimited numbers of European workers were able to cross borders, then so too could footballers, as wage earners.

From that point onwards, the number of European players in Spanish squads increased, which contributed to an increasing vision of football as a business, helped by hugely increased television contracts and other sponsorships. But that did not always mean a better team performance.

1999–2000: END OF THE NÚÑEZ ERA

The centenary celebrations were still ongoing and Van Gaal remained at the helm. The league campaign started brightly, but on Matchday Nine, Barça surrendered first place and then dropped as far as seventh in a topsy-turvy season that saw them eventually finish second, five points behind champions Deportivo de la Coruña. Carles Puyol made his debut that year, having come up through the ranks, in another demonstration of how the youth team was one of the club's strongest assets. Aside from his breakthrough, most people thought Van Gaal performed poorly in the transfer market, as did the team on the pitch.

The story of that season's *Copa del Rey* practically deserves its own chapter because Barça were eliminated in extraordinary circumstances. Atlético de Madrid comfortably prevailed in the first leg of the semi-final, 3–0. The second leg clashed with a Spain friendly, which meant that various players were away on international duty. Add in a few injuries, and it turned out Barça could not meet the minimum footballing requirements to field a team (the

competition specified that only three youth-team players could be selected). Barça had only 11 players, two of whom were goalkeepers. The team requested a date change, but this was denied and so on the day of the match, club captain Guardiola made his way out on to the pitch in an almost empty Camp Nou to inform the referee of the club's decision: it would not play a match that was impossible to contest on level terms.

The *Colchoneros* progressed to the final. Barça were banned from the following season's competition and fined 2m pesetas (12,000 euros), although this punishment would later be rescinded.

Despite breaking the record for goals scored in a Champions League campaign (45), the Catalan team was eliminated in the semi-finals by a magnificent Valencia side that won 4–1 at the Mestalla and lost 2–1 at the Camp Nou (5–3 on aggregate). That match was the final blow. The white handkerchiefs appeared again at the *Azulgrana* stadium, dedicated to both the coach and the president, who announced that he was leaving his post three days later. Núñez had said this before on other occasions, but this time he kept his promise. He did not even go to the ground to witness the team's final game from the directors' box, as he wanted to avoid another *pañolada* (the white handkerchief protest). Van Gaal also waived the two years remaining on his contract and departed for pastures new.

Little more could be done that year, and Barça ended up without a title. Before his departure, the president had a dig at the press, which he accused of creating a bad atmosphere. The Dutch coach seconded his words and came out with a sarcastic comment that would live long in the memory: "Friends in the press, I'm leaving. Congratulations."

At the time of Núñez's departure, the club's wealth was more than 1.2bn euros and there were

LEFT: Van Gaal is one of the most important Barça coaches in the last two decades. Not only did he put Cruyff's ideas into practice – something that he had already done at Ajax – but he also laid part of the fundamental framework which explains the club's recent success.

more than 1,500 Barcelona supporters' clubs throughout the world. The eternally loyal vice-president, Joan Gaspart, ran in the elections that took place in late July 2000. This entrepreneurial hotelier, who ran against publicist Lluís Bassat, won with a large enough margin to confirm that, in spite of everything, members would get continuity. His re-election meant that a man who liked to define himself as a "*boix noi* disguised as a board member" remained at the forefront of club management at a time when urgent renovation was needed both on and off the pitch. He would not be given the time, nor would he know how to do it, as he later ended up confessing.

2000–04: FIRING BLANKS

The first major disappointment for the fans in the 2000–01 season was the defection of Portuguese player Luís Figo. Presidential elections took place without members knowing that the Portuguese star was leaving the *Azulgranas* to join the Real Madrid ranks, an act for which *los culés* never forgave him. The Barcelona winger dug his own grave by claiming that the rumours claiming he had signed a pre-contractual agreement with Real Madrid were not true since he would never do such a thing, he would never join Barça's arch-rivals. But *Los Merengues* were also holding elections that year and one candidate, Florentino Pérez, promised to sign the Portuguese player if he won. Pérez was elected president against all the odds and he paid Barça 60m euros to meet the player's release clause just a few hours later. Figo then asked Gaspart to find a solution to the conflict so that he could stay at Barça, but the *Azulgrana* president rejected his proposal. In the eyes of the fans who idolized him, Figo had lied – and from that moment he was considered a traitor.

As for sporting matters, Barça appeared in first place in the UEFA coefficients ranking, despite their elimination from the Champions League, ahead of reigning champions Real Madrid. They also received recognition from the International Olympic Committee for their sporting and educational development and as a tribute to their first century of history.

Llorenç Serra Ferrer was then handed the reins as Barça coach. He had joined the club in 1997 thanks to his success at Betis and had been working with the youth team until that point. Serra felt that Mourinho's services were superfluous, so the Portuguese returned home to work as a coach for the first time, at Benfica.

Although Serra Ferrer was in theory a fan of Cruyff's attacking, attractive football, he was unable to work miracles. Barça spent heavily on signings, including 36m euros on Marc Overmars, the most expensive player in the club's history at the time, but one who did not quite meet expectations. The team's poor form, which left them as low as ninth in the table, led Gaspart to replace Serra before the season came to a close, though the Spaniard remained at the club for a further year.

With seven league games remaining, the ever-loyal Rexach once again took the reins. Yet the change of coach did not prevent the team from ending the season empty-handed, eliminated from the Champions League in November and suffering semi-final defeats in both the UEFA Cup, by Liverpool, and the *Copa del Rey*, by Celta de Vigo. The league campaign ended with a disappointing fourth-place finish, 17 points behind champions

Real Madrid. To top it all, third-division Balaguer beat the *Azulgranas* in the *Copa Catalunya* final.

With no titles to celebrate, that season is instead remembered as the one when Figo betrayed the club. During his first visit to the Camp Nou wearing the white of Real Madrid in October 2000, he received the most heated reception ever seen at the stadium. *Los culés* relentlessly whistled, booed and insulted the Portuguese winger from the moment he left his hotel until he returned to the capital. The man who was once Barcelona vice-captain was now faced with banners that branded him a money-grabber, a Judas, a liar and a mercenary. The stadium shuddered from the deafening whistling every time Figo touched the ball, with the noise reaching 110 decibels. Young defender Carles Puyol stuck to Figo like a leech even when Barça had the ball. "The Camp Nou leaves Figo deaf and Real Madrid limping" was the headline in *Marca* the following day, underlining what had occurred on the terraces and on the pitch – the match ended with a 2–0 victory for the *Azulgranas*.

Ex-*Azulgrana* goalkeeper Javier Urruticoechea died in a road accident on the same day (May 27) as Barça went down 1–0 at home to Oviedo. This sad news, combined with setbacks on the pitch, left the fans with only small victories to cling to, such as seeing off Valencia on the final day of the season to clinch fourth place and Champions League qualification for the following season. That victory came in particularly heart-stopping circumstances: Rivaldo's third goal to seal his hat trick, a spectacular bicycle kick from outside the area to make it 3–2, arrived just two minutes from time.

Guardiola would don the *Azulgrana* colours for the final time against Celta in the *Copa del Rey*, in what would be the final loss of the campaign for *los culés,* who went down 3–1 in the first leg and drew the second leg 1–1. That summer, after

nearly two decades at the club, the midfielder said his goodbyes and left for Brescia. He would not return "home" until June 2007, to take charge of the Barcelona B team.

Barça were more lost than ever at the end of that season. The woeful results were a consequence of mismanagement and poor decisions. The club's name, which had always been synonymous with *seny* (sense) and good practice, was now put into question both on and off the pitch.

The positive note from 2001 was the arrival of a small, introverted boy from Argentina in mid-February, who would train at the club's sporting school. Never before had such an event taken place involving such a young boy from such a faraway place. However, Rexach considered that the Rosario-born youngster's talent was worth pulling out all the stops for, and Gaspart, who had complete trust in the sporting director, approved the decision. From that moment, Lionel Messi became a part of the *Azulgrana* family.

That season, 2001–2002, can be summarized in just a few lines. Gaspart splashed the cash on new signings; the standout one was a very young Javier Saviola who, at 19 years old, was an investment for the future; Rexach continued at the helm of a team that found itself eliminated from all competitions; Valencia ran out league winners as Barcelona finished 11 points behind them in fourth, with their Champions League dream ruined by Real Madrid in the semi-finals. The worst piece of news from that campaign, however, would not arrive until May 17, when Barcelona icon László Kubala died. May was becoming a cruel month for the *Azulgranas*.

The 2002–03 campaign began and Gaspart still did not really know what to do to put an end to the lack of trophies. Standout new faces included the Argentinian Juan Riquelme on the pitch, and,

"The Camp Nou leaves Figo deaf and Real Madrid limping."
Marca

surprisingly, Van Gaal, who was back for a second stint in the dugout. Yet performances and results were so disastrous that he was replaced after 19 games, with Barça twelfth in the league. Serbian Radomir Antić managed to bring the team up to sixth, which is where they finished the season, another year without a title to offer the fans. They were eliminated by *Segunda B* outfit Novelda in the first round of the *Copa del Rey*, 3–2. The exception to the norm that season was a record-breaking Champions League campaign, in which the team won 11 consecutive matches, before falling at the hands of Turin's *Vecchia Signora*, Juventus (1–1 and 1–2). By then, Rivaldo had left for AC Milan on a free transfer and president Gaspart had handed in his resignation.

He was vastly experienced, and had been a vice-president who had followed even the most controversial orders from Núñez without qualms, but he did not know how to be a good president. One image encapsulated not only that season but his whole presidency: Camp Nou, December 2002; a struggling Sevilla side were the opponents. The result? Barça were crushed 3–0. The supporters thunderously booed the directors' box and more specifically the president, who stoically withstood the chiding, utterly crestfallen. The image epitomized defeat and loneliness. Elections were called for that summer. FC Barcelona needed a total overhaul in order for change to happen.

2003–08: THE VIRTUOUS CIRCLE
On June 13, 2003, with six candidates and the highest turnout in the club's history, Barça elected their new president, Joan Laporta. The young lawyer won with a considerable majority, leaving behind favourite Lluís Bassat. The members had made it clear that the club needed a root-and-branch overhaul, as promised by the president-

elect, who was one of the founders of the defunct opposition group *Elefant Blau*.

The young entrepreneurs working with Laporta knew that an economic redesign was needed to go alongside improvements on the pitch if they wanted to breathe new life into the club. For that to happen they outlined an economic concept named the "virtuous circle": in order to win titles, you need top players who can take the club to the forefront of the sport, and from there you invest the money generated to continue strengthening the team. The theory had won the voters over, now it was time to put it into practice.

After the new president's arrival, changes began, starting with the Joan Gamper Trophy, which became a chance to showcase the squad, spiced up with live musical performances.

By that time, the team's new star had joined the ranks, a player with an unforgettable smile, who would give *los culés* so much joy: Ronaldo de Assis – Ronaldinho, the *gaucho*. As an example of what was expected from this player, the daily newspaper *Mundo Deportivo* published an article claiming that even the ex-President of the Catalan *Generalitat*, Jordi Pujol, had told *Azulgrana* vice-president Sandro Rosell that "it would be very good to sign Ronaldinho for the morale of the Catalans." Around 25,000 fans attended his welcome presentation in July 2003 and witnessed him for the first time signing the *shaka*, the characteristic gesture with which he is now associated. Ronaldinho stole the fans' hearts from the outset with his stage presence and way of playing. He was the embodiment of the change that members and supporters had been waiting for after so many disappointing days.

Another of the objectives imposed by the new board was increasing member numbers by setting up a campaign named "The Big Challenge". They also created a prize draw called *Palco Abierto*

LEFT: Barcelona have shown throughout their history that they're a different club. A sample of it is their relationship with UNICEF, in which the club paid the international organization for the right to have their logo on the Barcelona shirt. Carles Puyol, the club's long-standing captain, also wears an armband with the *señera*.

"Yes, yes, yes, we're going to Paris."
Barcelona fans

(Open Directors' Box), which still takes place today and involves ten members being chosen monthly by a notary to attend a match at the Camp Nou in the Directors' Box. The option of allowing kit sponsorship was also passed for the first time in the club's history after a marketing rethink.

The board also decided to put an end to a scourge that had been imposing its violent presence at various grounds for a long time: *los ultras*. The club now stopped supporting those groups; previously they had enjoyed the support of both Núñez and Gaspart, which enabled them to hide their criminal activities behind their support for the team. *Los ultras* ended up without economic support or tickets, and getting rid of them from the stadium required a joint effort with the authorities responsible for public order.

The board also improved communications with members and supporters through the modernization of the club magazine and television channel, and increased efforts to bring fans to the ground. The new team needed support and the knowledge that it had a public to answer to and for whom it was committed to performing well.

Laporta appointed Txiki Begiristain as director of football and Frank Rijkaard as coach to take over the sporting reins. Giovanni van Bronckhorst, Rafa Márquez and Edgar Davids (the latter arrived in the January transfer window) all became *Azulgranas* alongside Ronaldinho. It was the end of the road for Riquelme, Frank de Boer, Gaizka Mendieta and Fabio Rochemback, among others.

The new Barça made its Camp Nou debut in the second game of the campaign against Sevilla at a rather unusual time: five past midnight. The ungodly hour was due to the players' international commitments. Barça had requested a Tuesday fixture, Sevilla insisted on a Wednesday. Barça ended up giving in but scheduled the match for Wednesday, at 00:05. The attendance was even

more surprising as 80,236 fans stayed up late to see the new Barça live. It ended 1–1 after a Ronaldinho screamer from outside the area unleashed euphoria on the terraces. It was known as the "gazpacho match" after the famous Spanish cold soup that was on the club menu.

But the team still did not enjoy a flourishing start to the season. Inconsistent *Azulgrana* performances left them in thirteenth place after 15 games. Zaragoza knocked them out of the *Copa del Rey* at the quarter-final stage and Celtic ended their UEFA Cup campaign in the last 16. Yet despite the slip-ups and demands to sack the coach from some sections of supporters, Laporta persevered with Rijkaard. Once past the halfway point of the season, the team enjoyed a spectacular recovery, in which they were victorious in 15 of the last 20 encounters, shooting them up to a respectable second-place finish behind Valencia and ahead of Real Madrid's *galácticos*. Ronaldinho received the player of the season award and so excitement, if not silverware, was back at the Camp Nou.

The 2004–05 season saw the arrival of new players such as Sylvinho, Deco, Ludovic Giuly, Henrik Larsson and, crucially, Samuel Eto'o, who signed after some torrid negotiations with Mallorca, where he played, and Real Madrid, to whom he was contracted. Of course, the debut that everybody remembers today from that campaign belonged to Messi, whose first league appearance came against Espanyol on October 16, 2004. His first goal was set up by Ronaldinho in a match against Albacete. The Argentinian celebrated on the back of the Brazilian, who was both his protector and friend. No one really knew that they were witnessing an historic moment.

The team started the season strongly, reaching top spot after six games and going on to become champions after five trophy-less years. Barça were

knocked out of the *Copa del Rey* early on, and Chelsea saw them off in the Champions League last 16, but the magic displayed by the squad won the fans over once again. Furthermore, Ronaldinho won the 2005 FIFA World Player of the Year award and the *Ballon d'Or*, Eto'o won the African *Ballon d'Or* and goalkeeper Victor Valdés received the Zamora Trophy for conceding the lowest number of goals. These were all signs that things were moving in the right direction. The new board also launched a new tradition: celebrating titles with a parade that ended up at the Camp Nou, a concept that the fans wholeheartedly embraced.

Although everything was starting to look up on the pitch, disagreements returned at board level and five directors resigned after disagreeing with Laporta on certain issues. One of them was Sandro Rosell, who was until then sporting vice-president.

The majority of squad changes in the 2005–06 season were linked to the youth team, causing financial expenditure to fall. The squad was well-developed and only a few adjustments were required to strengthen Rijkaard's project. Betis were defeated in the *Supercopa*, but a hesitant start to the league campaign, including too many draws, meant Barça had to wait until the twelfth game to reach top spot. Once there, however, the team's progress seemed unstoppable. The new side was producing such fabulous performances that something unprecedented happened on November 19, 2005 at the Bernabéu. Real Madrid fans rose to their feet to applaud Ronaldinho's performance in a match that the *Azulgranas* won 3–0. That year, Barça achieved the record for consecutive victories: 14 in *La Liga*, 19 in all competitions. Between October 22 and January 22, Barça were untouchable. This stunning run of form was finally interrupted by Zaragoza in the *Copa del Rey* quarter-finals with a 4–2 away defeat, from which they could not recover.

The league title was wrapped up with three games to spare, as it was impossible for second-placed Real Madrid to make up the 12-point deficit. Cameroonian Eto'o won the *Pichichi* with 26 goals. The most exciting moment of the season, however, was clinching a second Champions League title against Arsenal at the Stade de France. The chant *"Sí, sí, sí, nos vamos a París"* ("Yes, yes, yes, we're going to Paris") was heard in the streets and from balconies in the city after progress in preceding rounds against Chelsea, Benfica and AC Milan. Thousands of supporters made the trip to the French capital to witness their team come back from Sol Campbell's opener after 37 minutes. First Eto'o, after 76 minutes, and then Juliano Belletti, nine minutes from time, clinched the victory. The players' reception on their return to Barcelona was tremendous.

Everything seemed to be going like clockwork, even when Barça's own regulations forced the club to hold elections, because Laporta's first ten days in charge, June 20–30, 2003, were considered to be an entire season. There was no opposition. Laporta was the only candidate with the necessary number of signatures to stand and his position was ratified without an election. His project continued.

Some important plans started by the previous board were also finally completed. For example, the *Ciutad Esportiva Joan Gamper* (FC Barcelona's training ground and academy base) was inaugurated in June 2006. Member numbers also increased significantly to reach 150,000, an increase of almost 50 percent in just three years.

ABOVE: The 2006 Champions League final pitted Barcelona against Arsenal, two teams that were changing how football was played. Both liked to have possession at a time when the physical game tended to dominate. Carles Puyol could do a bit of both.

ABOVE: Lionel Messi's goal against Getafe on April 18, 2007 – a dribble from his own half, with startling similarities to Maradona's goal against England in the 1986 – put the Argentine on the world map. Curiously both Frank Rijkaard and Pep Guardiola told him that he should not score that type of goal too often but should focus on being closer to the opposition penalty area.

The club's media presence was also flourishing, as Barça was the first side to launch its own official YouTube channel.

The club's finances had also improved considerably – so much so that, instead of searching for a kit sponsor, the board reached an agreement with UNICEF by which the club would give it 1.5m euros every year for five years. The UN body would use the funds on mutually agreed projects. Furthermore, Barça offered their shirt, which had known nothing but the club's crest for 107 years, as a logo bearer for UNICEF in order to shine the spotlight on the fight for children's rights. So the club lost out on advertising revenue but gained far more in terms of their image – that of an organization supporting the most vulnerable. From that moment, Laporta's board reinforced the social side of the club via the Foundation, implementing various programmes that used football as a tool for social inclusion. The UNICEF logo was first seen in September 2006 in a Champions League match against Levski Sofia, which Barça won 5–0.

Although off-the-pitch matters were looking good, the tide was gradually turning against the team on the pitch. In 2006–07, Rijkaard no longer had his assistant and linchpin Ten Cate by his side to maintain order in the dressing room. A combination of complacency and ill-discipline started to leave its mark on the team.

FC Barcelona won the *Supercopa* and the *Campeonato de Catalunya* against Espanyol, but went down 3–0 in the European Super Cup to Sevilla, all at the start of the season. They let the Club World Cup slip through their grasp as Porto Alegre's Internacional ran out 1–0 winners in December. Rafa Benítez's Liverpool put an end to Barça's Champions League campaign on away goals (1–2 and 0–1) in the last 16 in March. And although Barça were league leaders, some unusual setbacks towards the end of the campaign saw Real Madrid draw level on points and clinch the title thanks to their superior head-to-head record (2–0 and 3–3). There were two reasons to remember the penultimate league game against Espanyol: the goal that Messi scored with his hand to make it 1–1, and Raúl Tamudo's equalizer at the death to make it 2–2, which practically handed *La Liga* to Real Madrid.

Samuel Eto'o had been on the sidelines for just over four months with a serious meniscus injury in his right knee, and now, on his return, he decided to make some controversial statements that clearly described the problems in the dressing room. He singled out Brazilian star Ronaldinho, although it was common knowledge that "the Gaucho" had recently been putting more effort into partying than taking matches and training seriously. Neither Frank Rijkaard nor Sandro Rosell escaped criticism (though he did not name the latter). He stated that the dressing room was split, with one half siding with the ex-president. The Cameroonian striker had opened Pandora's box, and the demons were freed.

Out of the seven titles for which Barcelona were competing, they clinched only one. Getafe sent them packing in the *Copa del Rey*, but one of the goals is still remembered today for being remarkably similar to Maradona's solo effort against England in the World Cup in 1986. It was scored by Lionel Messi, who was already starting to get people on their feet each time he touched the ball. Although the *Azulgranas* won that match 5–2, Getafe's unexpected comeback in the return leg (4–0) sent Barça crashing out. It was a debacle that made people suspect that something serious was happening to the team.

Yet everything continued as planned in the following season, 2007–08: the summer tour of Asia; new signings (Thierry Henry, Yaya Touré, Eric Abidal and Gaby Milito); departures (including van Bronckhorst, Giuly, Maxi López, Belletti, Motta, and Saviola – who joined Real Madrid), and the celebration of the Camp Nou's 50th anniversary.

So everything was done, except sealing titles. Barça had set out to win at least one, and fight for another "until the end", in the words of sporting director Txiki Begiristain. But it was not to be. The team was comfortably second after 15 games but dropped to third in the final stretch and finished 18 points behind Real Madrid, unacceptable for a squad brimming with stars. The supporters accused the players of being too nonchalant, and the white handkerchiefs returned during the final games at the Camp Nou.

Barça suffered elimination from the *Copa del Rey* and the Champions League in the semi-finals. Koeman's Valencia disposed of them in the *Copa* (1–1 and 3–2). A solitary, spectacular strike by Manchester United's Paul Scholes in the return leg ended the quest for European glory after a 0–0 draw in Barcelona. Expectations were not met, not even in the *Copa Catalunya* against Gimnàstic de Tarragona.

The end of the season demanded some radical, painful but necessary changes. The first was saying goodbye to the coach who had managed to entertain the fans with attractive and effective football. Frank Rijkaard had to abandon a sinking ship that, seemingly, needed only a few holes in the hull repaired and, above all, all its oarsmen to row in sync. That task belonged to the new coach, a Barcelona man through and through who was a beloved disciple of Cruyff: Pep Guardiola.

ABOVE: Frank Rijkaard's final home game in the dugout at the Camp Nou was against Mallorca on May 11, 2008.

*"To play for Barcelona at 20 isn't easy.
Winning and scoring goals bring
their own pressures ..."*
Ronaldo

LEFT: The Brazilian Ronaldo spent only one season at Barcelona, winning three titles, including the UEFA Cup Winners' Cup. The allure of *Serie A* at the time meant many stars had only fleeting careers in Spain. Blessed with incredible pace and an eye for goal, Ronaldo's contribution was significant. He scored the winning goal of the 1997 Cup Winners' Cup final against Paris Saint-Germain. This was Barça's fourth triumph in the UEFA Cup Winners' Cup.

BELOW: Luís Figo was one of those rare talents who dominated the game from the wing. The fans felt such a strong connection with him, and vice versa, that he ended up becoming club captain. Figo was part of a formidable attack which included Rivaldo and Patrick Kluivert. The Portuguese winger made 172 league appearances for Barcelona, scoring 30 goals. So how could Luís Figo have been so adored by the media and supporters and yet later leave in such acrimonious circumstances?

LEFT: The only goalscorer Ronaldo lifts the Cup Winners' Cup after Barcelona defeated Paris Saint-Germain 1–0 in the final in Rotterdam on May 14, 1997.

BELOW: Bobby Robson already knew that Louis van Gaal was going to replace him and that his role had to be decided. The person who battled hardest for Robson to stay was José Mourinho, his translator and assistant, who even confronted Van Gaal in defence of his boss. Impressed, the Dutchman ended up incorporating the Portuguese into his coaching staff.

"They told me I was going to take over. It was a huge surprise."
Louis van Gaal

Below: Dutchman Louis van Gaal took over as Barcelona coach in 1997 and has since said, "I had a meeting with Núñez [the president], Bobby Robson and José Mourinho and they told me I was going to take over. It was a huge surprise. To start with I would look after the academy, but there they gave me the first indication that I would actually coach the first team … Mourinho, who can't have known either, was fuming. When I saw how furious he was, I thought, 'This man has something'. That's exactly why I hired him." Van Gaal would go on to lead FC Barcelona to two *La Liga* titles and a *Copa del Rey* win. One of his first triumphs was overcoming Borussia Dortmund in the UEFA Super Cup in 1998.

LEFT: In the 1998–99 season, Barcelona boasted a team with intelligent and versatile players. Many of them have ended up becoming managers: Patrick Kluivert, Luis Enrique, Mauricio Pellegrino, Phillip Cocu, Sergi Barjuán and Boudewijn Zenden. The following season would see the departure of star player and fan favourite Luís Figo. Years later, Figo said: "The board didn't treat me well, I was furious. Even as days went by, I was still angry and irritated because they didn't value me."

ABOVE and RIGHT: Barcelona celebrated their centenary with a match against Brazil in April 1999. Romário and the other stars who featured in Brazil's World Cup final defeat in 1998 were all present. Barcelona player Rivaldo said he was happy to wear the *Azulgrana* jersey, but country won over club and he wore the yellow of the *Seleção*. The entertaining game finished 2-2, with goals from Ronaldo and Rivaldo (for Brazil) and Luis Enrique and Phillip Cocu (for Barcelona) The Catalan club have always had a close relationship with Brazil. Between the arrival of the pioneering Fausto Dos Santos in 1931 and Neymar in 2013, 28 Brazilians have joined the club, including Ronaldo, Romário, Rivaldo, Ronaldinho, Sylvinho and Dani Alvés.

BELOW: Brazillian attacking midfielder Rivaldo joined Barcelona in 1997 and scored an impressive 19 goals in 34 games in his first *La Liga* to finish the competition's second-placed top scorer. A key figure in Barça's 1997–98 and 1998–99 *La Liga* title triumphs, he was voted FIFA World Player of the Year in 1999. In his third season, Rivaldo fell out with Van Gaal over the coach's insistence on playing him on the left wing.

RIGHT: Rivaldo was always a player who could rise for the big occasion. In June 2001, Barcelona had to beat Valencia on the final day of the season to leapfrog them and qualify for the Champions League. Rivaldo stepped up and scored a spectacular hat trick. His third goal was a perfectly delivered bicycle kick from the edge of the box at the death. Carles Puyol jumps for joy as Rivaldo rips his shirt off in celebration following his spectacular third goal.

"19 November 2005: The Day Barcelona Left the Bernabéu to Applause."
Marca

LEFT: Ronaldinho's arrival in July 2003 represented a turning point in Barcelona's history as smiles returned to the club. The Brazilian arrived even though Joan Laporta had an agreement in place with Manchester United over the signing of David Beckham.

BELOW: Ronaldinho put in some majestic performances against Real Madrid. Here he takes a free kick, one of his specialities, at the Bernabéu in April 2004. The *Merengue* supporters even applauded his performance in 2005–06, which had only previously happened to Maradona. It was reported in the Madrid newspaper *Marca as* "19 November 2005: The Day Barcelona Left the Bernabéu to Applause."

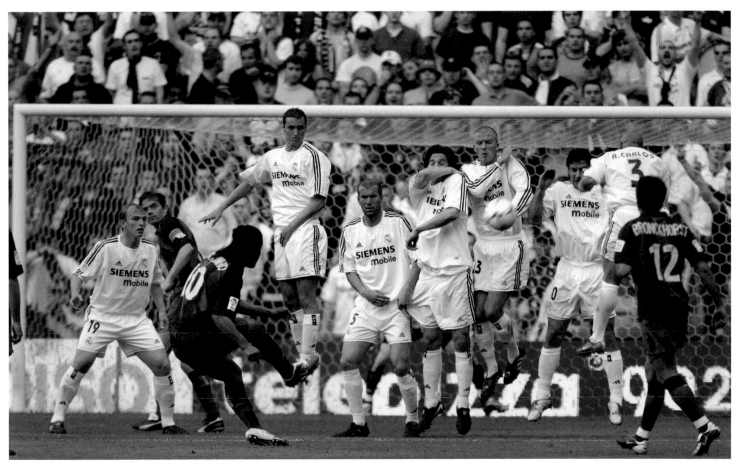

BELOW: The Stade de France, Paris, in May 2006 saw a thrilling Champions League final between two of Europe's great footballing sides. Barcelona needed two late goals against Arsenal, whose goalkeeper, Jens Lehmann, had been sent off after 18 minutes. Sol Campbell's first-half header was eventually cancelled out by Samuel Eto'o before Juliano Belletti hit the winner in the final 15 minutes.

RIGHT: Barcelona captain Carles Puyol lifts the Champions League trophy surrounded by Maxi López, Giovanni van Bronckhorst, Juliano Belletti and Ronaldinho. It was Barcelona's second Champions League triumph. Frank Rijkaard said of the win, "The players have done a great job. The key to success has been unity, from the players to the coaching staff, the board and the rest of the club's employees."

FOLLOWING PAGES: Two magical years saw two *La Liga* triumphs (2004–05 and 2005–06) and the club's second European Cup. The world, the club and even Rijkaard believed that a new era had begun. But the hardest thing of all is staying at the top.

RONALDO

It all happened in a flash. Just one season, as with fellow Brazilian Romário, was sufficient for his play to seduce *los culés* and, by extension, all true football fans. The striker, who had an impressive physique, was pure magic according to all football experts, who consider him one of the best players of all time.

Born in Rio de Janeiro, Brazil in 1976, Ronaldo arrived at FC Barcelona from PSV Eindhoven, where he had already amply demonstrated his goalscoring ability aged just 19. His statistics preceded him, since he had scored 42 goals in 46 outings during two seasons at the Dutch club. Furthermore, he was already starting to become an international star, prompting FC Barcelona to pay 2.5bn pesetas (just over 15m euros) for him, a record transfer fee at the time.

Ronaldo was a striker with a unique technique, using a burst of pace to get past opponents before using his extraordinary natural finishing ability to put the ball in the goal. During his solitary season at Barcelona, he passed the goalscoring test with flying colours by netting 47 times in 51 matches, demonstrating that the money spent on him was worth it. His short stay at the club under Sir Bobby Robson included victories in the Cup Winners' Cup, *Copa del Rey* and *Supercopa*.

His name reached all corners of the globe in an *Azulgrana* shirt, with unforgettable goals such as the one against Compostela in October 1996, which he has declared his favourite. He picked the ball up in his own half and dodged tackles from various defenders before calmly slotting home from inside the area in a demonstration of ability, strength, speed and power. This goal, which generated applause even from opposition fans, established him as the new Pelé.

He was still only 20 years old and had a promising future at the Catalan club, but this was cut short by a breakdown in communication with the board when it came to renegotiating his contract. Inter Milan were willing to meet his release clause, which amounted to 4bn pesetas [24m euros], another record. Barça lost a star who had treated the club to some glorious moments and, while doing so, had won the FIFA World Player of the Year award, as well as becoming a *Copa América* champion with the Brazilian national team.

Later, he shone at the World Cup in France in 1998, in which Brazil finished runners-up, and he was the star of the World Cup in Japan and South Korea in 2002, where he scored a brace in the final against Germany. Following a lengthy summer soap opera, he joined Real Madrid for the 2002–03 season, becoming part of a team that became known as the *Galácticos* because of the superstars playing there.

"If I was asked about my wildest dreams, I would have never considered this."
Ronaldo

LUÍS FIGO

It could have been a story of eternal love, but circumstances dictated that it would end in a most tempestuous divorce. Luís Filipe Madeira Caeiro Figo, known as Figo, was born in Lisbon, Portugal, in 1972 and arrived at Johan Cruyff's FC Barcelona from Sporting Lisbon in the 1995–96 season. During his five years as an *Azulgrana*, he won two league titles, two *Copas del Rey*, one European Super Cup, one *Supercopa* and one Cup Winners' Cup.

He wore the captain's armband when Guardiola was not playing, and *los culés* idolized him. He played under three coaches who were all vastly different in terms of style, play and personality: Cruyff, Robson and Van Gaal. He showed his professionalism and ability to adapt to all of them. His play made him the worthy winner of several awards: the best player in Portugal in 1995 and 1996, the best player in *La Liga* 1999–2000 (when still at FC Barcelona), the *Ballon d'Or* in 2000 and the FIFA World Player of the Year 2001. He finished third with Portugal at Euro 2000, runner-up in 2004 and fourth in the World Cup in 2006. He was crucial in the 1997 *Copa del Rey* success, as his brace in the final helped Barça defeat Betis 3–2.

However, all the good moments were eclipsed in the minds of *barcelonistas* by one simple fact: he joined Real Madrid. Others had done it before him, yet Figo's departure was treated as absolute treachery, and from loving him unconditionally one minute, he was vilified by the fans like nobody before him the next.

It was election time at Real Madrid. Florentino Pérez was running for the presidency and one of his promises was to bring Figo to the club. Pérez signed a pre-contract with the player's agent, containing a 5bn pesetas [20m euros] penalty clause if the midfielder backtracked on the deal. This allowed Perez to promise that if Figo did not sign for Real Madrid, he would pay for all 70,000 Real Madrid season-ticket holders' renewals the following season.

The *Azulgrana* side took it for granted that Figo would stay. "He will not go," said everybody that mattered at Barcelona. President Núñez, who was about to leave his post, paid no attention to the Portuguese winger's demands, thinking that he simply wanted to improve his contract. In Figo's words, even when Florentino Pérez's offer arrived, Barcelona still thought that he just wanted to negotiate his wages, confused by the fact that Figo kept repeatedly reassuring the media that he was staying at Barcelona. Pérez won the elections, paid 15bn pesetas [60m euros], which was a world transfer record at the time, and Figo joined a squad that would end up being known as the *galácticos*. *Los culés* never forgave him.

His first match for Madrid at the Camp Nou is remembered as the worst reception a player has ever received at the ground. On another occasion in 2002, each time the Portuguese player tried to take a corner the Camp Nou spectators bombarded him with all types of objects, including bottles, snooker balls, mobile phones and even a pig's head.

" You cannot erase history. My conscience is clear."
Luís Figo

RONALDINHO

They used to call Ronaldinho the player who gave Barça their smile back, and this magical footballer captivated the fans with his *jogo bonito*. He left his mark on the five seasons that he spent at the *Azulgranas* by contributing decisively to two *La Liga* championships, one Champions League (the club's second), two *Supercopas* and three *Copas Catalunya*.

Born in Porto Alegre, Brazil in 1980, Ronaldinho was another of the brilliant Brazilians, such as Ronaldo, Rivaldo and Romário, who lit up Spanish grounds with their performances. He arrived at Barça from Paris Saint-Germain in July 2003, to form part of Frank Rijkaard's new project.

He was already a World Cup winner, having represented his country in various matches at the tournament in Japan and South Korea in 2002, including the quarter-final against England, in which he netted the winning goal. He instantly blew people away with his hugely imaginative style of play that put a smile on fans' faces. He was both a goalscorer, with 94 goals, and a creator. His performances aroused so much admiration that the ovation he received at the Bernabéu from the *Merengues* after scoring a brace against Real Madrid in October 2005 is still remembered today. He received his second FIFA World Player of the Year award, as well as the *Ballon d'Or*, in the same year. And his wonder goal against Sevilla was so rapturously celebrated that the city's seismographs recorded small tremors.

The world's best player at the time was famous for his chips, *espaldinhas* (touches with his back), bicycle kicks and the "cow tail" turn made popular by Romário. He could even pass to himself.

Guardiola and Messi unanimously praised him and stated that "Ronni" changed Barcelona's style of play with his mentality and enthusiasm. Furthermore, Messi has always been grateful to the Brazilian for welcoming him into the first team when he arrived. Ronaldinho became Messi's protector and teacher in their first few years together. "The Gaucho" was a generous player who provided the Argentinian with two assists in a row, allowing him to score his first two goals for Barça (although the first was ruled out for offside).

However, the days when the joker's mischievous smile lit up the team became less and less frequent. In his final two seasons as an *Azulgrana*, Ronaldinho started to show signs of being excessively relaxed, which led to him having to seek pastures new when Guardiola arrived in the dugout.

He was transferred to AC Milan for 25m euros in summer 2008, which worked in Messi's favour the following season as the Argentinian truly came into his own. Eto'o was kept for another year, although Guardiola had originally asked for his departure as well. Ronaldinho returned to Brazil to play for Atlético Mineiro, having accumulated a vast number of both team and personal accolades.

"Football is about joy. It's about dribbling."
Ronaldinho

6. 2008–2014: GUARDIOLA AND THE GLORY YEARS

Pep Guardiola's only previous coaching experience was at FC Barcelona B. In 2007, Barcelona's sporting director, Txiki Begiristain, offered him the role of youth team coordinator, but Guardiola turned it down, stating that he wanted to be a coach. However, there was no space for him in the first team, so he consequently asked if he could coach Barça B, much to Begiristain's surprise. He was then handed the reins of the Third Division side and in one year achieved a miracle, by winning the championship and sealing promotion to *Segunda B*. Those were his credentials.

Halfway through the 2007–08 season, while the pressure was building on Rijkaard, some, including Johan Cruyff, were already suggesting that the former central midfielder should become the next coach. Others believed that only one man would know how to establish order in the midst of chaos: José Mourinho. Although appointing him would have involved a loss of identity in terms of style of play, some did not mind, provided that the team came out of their rut.

Begiristain and Marc Ingla, that season's vice-president in charge of football matters, thought that such a crucial decision should be made by the same process used by bosses in big companies when choosing key staff: first draw up a profile of the ideal candidate and then conduct various interviews to find the person who best fits. Among other qualities, Barça were looking for a coach who respected the style of play inherited from Rijkaard (who had himself inherited it from Cruyff), a coach who could actively manage the dressing room and a coach who respected all opponents. A long list was whittled down to just three names: Ernesto Valverde, José Mourinho and Guardiola. But the only one who really met the club's prerequisites was the latter, a former player and a Catalan (he was born in Santpedor). He lived and breathed the club's colours and was fully aware of its values, relevance and history.

Some board members preferred Mourinho, whom they considered a potential tool to increase the value of the Barça brand. Even Begiristain and Ingla were impressed by the first face-to-face interview that they had with the Portuguese coach. However, they were not convinced by Mourinho's public face and his way of dealing with the press. Furthermore, Begiristain maintained that Guardiola's inexperience would not be a problem. He had closely followed the progress made by the B team under Guardiola's management; and he had witnessed how Guardoila applied certain strategies and techniques, as well as formation variations, including occasionally reverting to 3–4–3, which had not been seen since the Cruyff and van Gaal days. He was convinced that the former player would know how to lead the first team with professionalism, enthusiasm and commitment.

However, very few strongly agreed with Barça's sporting director at the time, although Cruyff and Evarist Murtra, a director and personal friend of Guardiola, were on his side. In order to appoint Guardiola, president Laporta needed convincing. He felt indebted to Rijkaard for the good times and the titles that he had earned for the club, but eventually agreed to give Guardiola his chance. He informed Guardiola during a dinner made famous by the coach's spontaneous response on hearing the proposal: "You wouldn't have the balls to do that!" In the meantime, however, everything hinged on whether or not Rijkaard, still in position, could lead the team to the Champions League final.

Rijkaard came up short, and his era came to an end. Guardiola took over at the end of that season, an appointment he kept secret until the club made it public. Without knowing it, *los culés* were about to enter their most glorious period, both in terms of titles won and the breath-taking quality of their performances.

PREVIOUS PAGES:
Pedro holds the 2011 Champions League trophy aloft as supporters and team-mates look on. The final against Manchester United was played at Wembley.

LEFT: Pep Guardiola's official unveiling as Barcelona coach took place on August 16, 2008, during the 43rd Joan Gamper Trophy, before a friendly match against Boca Juniors.

RIGHT: Tito Vilanova gives instructions during the second leg of the Champions League quarter-final against Bayern Munich on April 14, 2009. The influential Vilanova sadly lost his two-year battle with cancer on April 25, 2014.

2008–09: BARÇA'S SIX CUPS

June 17, at the Camp Nou's Sala París, 37-year-old Pep Guardiola is officially unveiled as FC Barcelona's new first-team coach.

Barça really got people talking that summer. On the pitch, not many people seemed to believe in the new coach, whose credentials as a brilliant player could not mask his inexperience as a coach. In the boardroom, Laporta survived a vote of no-confidence by the skin of his teeth.

Just like at Barça B, Guardiola's Number Two was his friend, Tito Vilanova, an exceptional analyst of teams and matches. Various changes needed to take place in order for the team to function once again, including an unpleasant and unavoidable dressing-room clear-out. One of the first to depart was Ronaldinho, the Brazilian superstar who had provided the fans with so much entertainment until his decline. Nor was he the only one who had to leave. Deco, Edmilson, Gianluca Zambrotta, Lilian Thuram and Giovanni dos Santos also left the club. Eto'o was on the verge of joining them, as Guardiola announced in a press conference.

The coach knew what type of team he wanted and the type of players that would fit in. At the time he believed that Eto'o's strong personality and rebellious nature did not match what he had in mind for the group. But once the Cameroonian was freed from Ronaldinho and Deco's influence, he started to respect his new coach's orders and, in turn, earned the recognition that his excellent play deserved. An extraordinary pre-season and

a request by some of his team-mates secured his future; Guardiola kept him for another season.

To replace those who sought pastures new, Dani Alves, Martin Cáceres, Seydou Keita, Alexander Hleb and Gerard Piqué arrived. The latter had to be claimed back from Manchester United, having come through the Barcelona youth ranks alongside Cesc Fàbregas and Lionel Messi.

The Catalan coach decided from the start that he did not need one single man to carry the team; instead he wanted a team that would earn the fans' respect by working hard and which was composed of players, some of whom were still very young, who had gradually worked their way up through the youth system. They needed to live and breathe FC Barcelona and be spokesmen for the club's values. The group was comprised of Carles Puyol, Xavi Hernández, Andrès Iniesta and Messi, all of whom had been previously forced to take a back seat.

That year, the youth-team disciples were joined by Pedro, Sergio Busquets and Thiago Alcántara, all of whom had already played under Guardiola in the youth team. Pedro and Busquets would make a sizeable contribution to Spain's first-ever World Cup triumph just one year later in 2010.

It is undeniable that part of Guardiola's success is linked to his personality and communication skills. All of those present at his first team talk in St Andrews, Scotland, during the 2008–09 pre-season were blown away. From everything that he said that day, one sentence stood out: "I could forgive any mistake, but I will not forgive anyone

> ### *"Fasten your seatbelts, we're going on a fun ride."*
> ## Pep Guardiola

who doesn't give his heart and soul to Barcelona." He made it clear that he wanted his players to give it their all and return to a culture of effort and teamwork. He did not want little groups, cliques, press leaks or excuses after a poor performance. He wanted commitment, fight, discipline, unity and confidence in a project that they had to move forward as a collective. His talk set the foundation of what was to come.

Guardiola wanted a camaraderie among all the players, which is why he insisted on them speaking only Spanish or Catalan. He also arranged for everybody to mix in the dining hall in order to avoid the creation of closed groups. There was a whole series of similar rules, with sanctions for the rule-breakers. It very quickly became a natural way for players to interact, despite some initial reluctance, mainly from veteran and foreign players. The Catalan coach wanted his players to feel more like the club's employees than stars, so he organized training sessions away from the beady eyes of the press and supporters. The players were forced to concentrate on their jobs without interference or distraction. One more change: no more pre-match meetings in hotels in the days leading up to games, which took some getting used to, but many players were thankful when they saw how it decreased stress levels.

"I cannot promise titles, but I am convinced the supporters will be proud of us," said Guardiola. Just as Cruyff did in his first year, he made a commitment to fill the terraces once again, and guaranteed a style of play that *los culés* would recognize and enjoy, rather than guaranteeing trophies. "Fasten your seatbelts, we're going on a fun ride," he announced to a packed Camp Nou during his unveiling on August 16, 2008. And boy, did he deliver on his promise.

The parallels with Cruyff would be seen on many other occasions. Guardiola said many times that the Dutch coach was a huge inspiration, thanks to his way of approaching matches and football in general. "We are almost like disciples of the principle that Cruyff founded here," he wrote on one occasion, without underplaying what he had taken from another team which had also captivated him, Van Gaal's Ajax.

The keys to the style that provided Barcelona with so much success were based on methods previously established by Michels, Cruyff, Van Gaal and Rijkaard, which the Catalan coach perfected. The first, and fundamental, key was possession and ball control. As Guardiola said himself: "In the football world there is only one secret: either I have the ball or I don't have it." He decided that his team would want to have it. The second key was trying not to lose possession, at least not from mistakes. The third, but no less important, key was collective pressing near the opponents' penalty area, something that had already occurred under Rijkaard but which became a fundamental premise under Guardiola. He also called upon a Van Gaal teaching: if you lose the ball, there is a five-second margin to get it back before dropping off.

The new coach's first challenge was to achieve Champions League qualification against Wisła Kraków, because Barça had finished only third in *La Liga* the previous season. Some of Guardiola's changes could already be seen in those matches. The defenders would start the build-up: the centre-backs and goalkeeper became the first line of attack. The team would push up thanks to its attacking full-backs and increased ball circulation. That, combined with greater player movement, helped to create more space. Of course, Guardiola had something that other teams did not: a squad of exceptional quality. The players also had something that was not very common: a coach who explained the reasons for his instructions, so that they knew why they had to follow them. Barça

RIGHT: Lionel Messi celebrates his second goal (Barcelona's fifth) in the 2–6 league victory over Real Madrid at the Bernabéu on May 2, 2009.

breezed through the qualifier with a convincing 4–0 victory away, although they suffered a narrow defeat in the return leg.

The first league match against newly promoted Numancia arrived. Barça dominated and had 20 efforts on goal, but out of only three chances that the modest team from Soriano had, one went in. Barça slumped to a 1–0 defeat. This was a tough blow from which they had to recover quickly. Guardiola's first move was to remind everyone not to lose sight of the main aim: to develop a certain style of play, despite that night's setback.

Their second league outing was against a very defensive Racing Santander at the Camp Nou, in which the *Azulgranas* could not find a winning goal. There was still some polishing off to do, but in general the team had responded to what the coach had asked of them. Just some patience was needed, exactly what some sections of the press didn't have, as Barça temporarily sat in the relegation zone. "Guardiola is too weak, he has no personality, Mourinho would have been better…" said the Catalan press.

Barça finally came out victorious in their third game after putting six goals past a Sporting de Gijón side that was blown away by the *Azulgranas'* pressing and rhythm. They would not taste defeat again until December 9 against Shakhtar Donetsk in the Champions League, finding a rich vein of form in which there were only two draws, against Basle and Getafe. In fact, the slip-up against Numancia was the solitary *La Liga* defeat in a record-breaking first half of the

season in which they ended up with 50 points. Barça were top after nine games, and would not relinquish their position all season.

Not only did the supporters make peace with the team thanks to the victories, but they also witnessed some of the best footballing moments in the club's history. Of course the results were pleasing, but the true highlight was the spectacle. That year Barça and, by extension, football in general, earned quite a few new followers. Even the *New York Times* dedicated an article to the club in December 2008, which reported that "For some, watching FC Barcelona play soccer these days is akin to reading a book that is hard to put down." The journalist finished off by saying, "Style is the name of the game at Barcelona."

Of course, if you ask *los culés* which match they will forever remember from that season, without doubt the most popular answer would be the 6–2 drubbing of Real Madrid at the Bernabéu. It was an historic feat achieved by a majestic performance. The date was May 2, five league games remained, Juande Ramos's Real Madrid were enjoying a rich vein of form and only four points separated the two teams. Victory was essential for Barça to tie up the league title. They had already beaten *Los Merengues* 2–0 at the Camp Nou, but an away win would truly exceed all expectations. Barça dominated from the outset, but the opener was scored by Madrid's Gonzalo Higuaín before the *Azulgranas* took control. Henry, Puyol and Messi netted the next three. Sergio Ramos brought Real Madrid back into the contest

"I cannot promise titles, but I am convinced the supporters will be proud of us."
Pep Guardiola

with a goal in the 56th minute, but Henry bagged his second just two minutes later. Another Messi strike and a Piqué goal finished off a tremendous, unforgettable night for *los culés*.

MAY 2009: A ROLLERCOASTER

May would turn out to be a rollercoaster that both players and supporters would never forget. Good league form was accompanied by an impressive Champions League run that led them to Stamford Bridge, just four days after the *clásico*. Chelsea had held Barça to a 0–0 stalemate in the first leg; a place in the final was at stake. The Blues opened the scoring after nine minutes and when almost everybody had given up hope of a miracle, up popped Iniesta to score a stunning goal in stoppage time to book ten-man Barcelona their place in the final.

Hardly one week later, on May 13, Barcelona defeated Athletic Bilbao 4–1 at the Mestalla, clinching their first trophy of the season, the *Copa del Rey*. It started a domino effect. Four days later, Barça were crowned league champions. Ten days later, Manchester United were outplayed in the Champions League final in Rome, going down 2–0 as the *Azulgranas* lifted their third Champions League trophy. Barça and *los culés* were over the moon after sealing the treble.

As mentioned, it wasn't just the titles themselves, it was the performances to clinch them that earned global admiration from football supporters. Guardiola used ideas from earlier generations and adjusted and adapted them to suit the times. He maintained the same model and spirit, but opened up previously unimaginable possibilities. He had no fear in making the changes he deemed necessary along the way. Journalist John Carlin wrote for the Barça magazine: "After seeing them play I could finally understand what Bobby Robson and I could not 12 years ago:

you need to aim as high as possible, you need to dream because in football, just like in everything else, you need to be highly ambitious."

There was just one way for other teams to contend with the hungry animal that FC Barcelona had become: set up a very tight, stifling defence and wait for a mistake in order to launch a counterattack. During the first year, very few knew that it was the only option. But Chelsea did it in the Champions League semi-final, and the technique would have succeeded had it not been for Iniesta's equalizer, which rewarded Barça's attacking impetus and good play.

It should be remembered that the club's four captains that season all received their football education at La Masía: Xavi, Puyol, Victor Valdés and Iniesta. In Rome, seven of the 11 starters had come up through the ranks, almost fulfilling a dream of a team made up of 11 *"canteranos"* (kids from the lower ranks), which Van Gaal had expressed in 2000 – to the disbelief of many. This was a team packed full of stars who worked as hard as any. One of them, Messi, was awarded his first *Ballon d'Or* that year, while Xavi came third.

2009–10: TITLES GALORE

The 2008–09 campaign had come to a close, but there was still time for more trophies in the calendar year. To begin with, Barça convincingly won the *Supercopa* against Athletic Bilbao in August, 5–1 on aggregate. An extra-time Pedro goal was sufficient to beat Shakhtar Donetsk in the European Super Cup five days later. The only title that still eluded them was finally won in December: the Club World Cup. The opposition was Estudiantes from La Plata, who were defeated by a single Messi strike in extra time. Six titles in one year – a record that no other team had ever achieved. Guardiola could not hold back the tears after that sixth success.

ABOVE: In the gardens at *La Masía*, Sandro Rosell makes his inaugural speech having been elected president on July 1, 2010, and promises the club will enter a "golden era".

The difficult part would be maintaining such high standards. In an effort to do so, Guardiola made some changes to the squad. Zlatan Ibrahimović and Maxwell arrived from Inter Milan. Samuel Eto'o went the other way after five trophy-filled years at the Camp Nou. The Swede was bought for a cost of 45m euros plus Eto'o (whose valuation was around 20m euros) and a further 3m euros that had to be paid to Inter because of an agreement over a loan deal for Belarussian Hleb, who eventually went to Stuttgart. The final total was 68m euros, a club record at the time. Even with the new signings, Barcelona were unable to overcome both Sevilla in the *Copa del Rey* last 16 (1–2 and 0–1) and Inter in the Champions League semi-final (3–1 and 1–0). Their unstoppable league form continued, however, as they were league leaders after four games and would relinquish their position only on a couple of occasions. Their 20th league title was lifted on May 16 with a record points tally of 99.

Meanwhile, off-the-pitch activities also caught the fans' attention. The club's good image – thanks to its style of play, but also social action, such as the agreement with UNICEF – contributed to both an extraordinary economic recovery at the club and a spectacular rise in member numbers. In terms of revenue, FC Barcelona was second in the "rich list" of world clubs, and it boasted more than 173,000 members. The dominating news from that summer, however, was the election of a new president. Laporta was unable to stand (club regulations dictate a maximum of two terms

in office) and Sandro Rosell came out victorious. Laporta's former ally took up office on June 13, 2010 with 61.35 percent of the votes.

2010–11: ANOTHER TREBLE

Spain lifted the World Cup for the first time that summer in South Africa, with seven Barcelona players in the starting line-up, six of whom had passed through the doors of *La Masía*. All experts agreed that the national style of play bore Barça's hallmark.

The season began with the departures of Dmytro Chygrynskiy – signed the previous year but who had not produced as expected on the pitch – Yaya Touré, Thierry Henry and Rafael Márquez. The most talked-about move, however, was Zlatan Ibrahimović's loan deal to AC Milan, after the Swede's heated arguments with his coach. Standout new arrivals included the forward from Asturias, David Villa, and Adriano and Javier Mascherano. An effort was made to bring back youth-team disciple and Arsenal captain Cesc Fàbregas, but no agreement was reached even though the player expressed his desire to play alongside his old team-mates.

The Joan Gamper Trophy took on special meaning that season as Ronaldinho's AC Milan were the opponents. 97,000 spectators witnessed the special reception that the ex-*Azulgrana* received before posing with the Barça team for a photo. Although his old team won the match on penalties, "the Gaucho" was presented with the trophy in front of a cheerful Camp Nou crowd.

> *"... watching FC Barcelona play soccer these days is akin to reading a book that is hard to put down ... Style is the name of the game at Barcelona.*
> **New York Times**

A 3–1 first-leg defeat at Sevilla in the *Supercopa* did not prevent Barcelona from bringing home the first silverware of the season as a Messi hat trick at the Camp Nou helped the *Azulgranas* to a stunning 4–0 victory.

It was José Mourinho's first year in the Real Madrid dugout and he became a key figure in the rivalry between the sides, which reached an entirely new level. The Portuguese coach's less attractive, yet equally effective, football put Guardiola's style of play into question. Well, almost. In a season of five *clásicos*, the first one was played in November 2010 and a five-star performance by Barça left some describing it as the best in the club's history.

That year's *Ballon d'Or* finalists were announced in December, which was considered a clear demonstration of the hard work behind the scenes at the club's football school, because all three finalists had received their footballing education at La Masía. Messi received the award for the second time, ahead of Iniesta and Xavi, who made his second appearance on the podium.

While Barça continued their march towards the league title, the season's second *clásico* ended 1–1 on April 16. Four days later, Real Madrid lifted the *Copa del Rey* after a single extra-time header by Cristiano Ronaldo. With hardly any time to digest the various games, the fourth *clásico* arrived on April 27, which pitted the arch-rivals against each other in the Champions League semi-final. Barça ran out 2–0 winners at the Bernabéu after two more Messi goals, one of which was a superb solo effort. Both matches were more heated than usual, which was supposedly part of Mourinho's strategy. They were riddled with incident, such as the touchline scuffle straight after the half-time whistle in the first leg, claims by Real Madrid coaches that referees were biased towards FC Barcelona (Pepe's red card in

the first leg and Higuaín's disallowed goal in the return) and Mourinho's press conference after the first game in which he brought Barcelona's victories into question, including their previous Champions League triumph.

Mourinho, revelling in his role as the villain, made the atmosphere extremely tense at the *clásicos* during the years in which he overlapped with Guardiola. *Los Blancos* pinned their hopes on him, thanks to his media performances that made him the perfect enemy for *los culés*, who would sing "Mourinho, stay put" during each Real Madrid defeat at the Camp Nou. Many thought that the Portuguese's arrival in Spain made *La Liga* into a type of comedy sketch that encouraged even less competition at the top of the table. For others, Guardiola included, this battle between the giants started to become unbearable because it detracted from footballing matters. And so the Catalan expressed himself with frustration in a press conference before Real Madrid's elimination from the competition: in the press room, Mourinho was "the f*****g boss". Yet Barça's superiority continued to be shown on the pitch, for which they continued to be praised by the press – except for Madrid-based journalists, of course – and the supporters. They were lauded even more after winning a third consecutive league title and reaching the Champions League final. Guardiola returned to Wembley, the stadium where Barça had won their first-ever European Cup.

Europe's best two sides at the time met on May 28, 2011 in a battle of two opposing views on how to play the same game. Barça and Manchester United arrived on a level footing in almost everything: both had already held the title three times, and their head-to-head record until then was three wins each and four draws. That day, something had to give, and a clearly superior Barça ended up convincing even the most

ABOVE: Andrés Iniesta and Neymar battle for the ball during the FIFA Club World Cup final on December 18, 2011 in Yokohama, Japan. Barça ran out 4–0 winners over Santos with goals from Xavi, Fàbregas and Messi (two).

PREVIOUS PAGES:
Messi, *Ballon d'Or* 2010 winner, with runner-up Iniesta on the left and third-placed Xavi on the right. The Camp Nou crowd were shown the trophy before the *Copa del Rey* clash against Betis on January 12, 2011, which Barça won handsomely, 5–0.

sceptical viewers with an emphatic 3–1 victory. Pedro, Messi and Villa were the goalscoring heroes while Rooney netted for United.

Eric Abidal, who had had a cancerous tumour removed from his liver, had already played the last two minutes of the semi-final against Real Madrid just seven weeks after the operation. Not only did he now play the whole final, but he became an important source of inspiration for his team-mates. Captain Puyol, who entered the fray with two minutes remaining to finish off the match, insisted that the Frenchman lift the cup, crowning off one of the most emotional moments experienced in Barça's long history.

In case everything that Guardiola's team had achieved was not enough, it must be remembered that the season began soon after the World Cup in South Africa came to a close. Eight *Azulgranas* were in the victorious Spain ranks and various other internationals also competed, with hardly any time to recharge their batteries.

2011–12: CUPS BUT NO LEAGUE
FC Barcelona opened the season by beating Real Madrid in the *Supercopa* (2–2 in the first and 3–2 in the second leg) and Porto 2–0 in the European Super Cup. One of the new star signings that season, Chilean Alexis Sánchez, would feature in two of those matches. The player whose arrival *los culés* were most eagerly awaiting, however, was midfielder Cesc Fàbregas, who returned home that year. Other new additions – Isaac Cuenca,

Christian Tello and Rafinha among others – came from Barcelona B. Bojan Krkić, Gabi Milito and Jeffren were shown the door and Ibrahimović sealed a permanent move to AC Milan.

FC Barcelona clinched their second Club World Cup in December after demolishing Neymar and Brazil's Santos 4–0, the goals coming from Messi (twice), Fàbregas and Xavi. Before the end of the winter break on January 9, Leo Messi received his third *Ballon d'Or* and Xavi had to settle for bronze for a third straight year. Guardiola also received recognition for his managerial achievements as that year's jury deemed him the best coach in the world, ahead of Sir Alex Ferguson and José Mourinho.

The 2012 Champions League escaped their grasp in the semi-finals against Chelsea, despite outstanding performances such as the 7–1 annihilation of Bayer Leverkusen in the last-16 second leg (an astounding 10–2 on aggregate) with five Messi goals and a Tello brace. Three days after Champions League elimination, Guardiola (exhausted, and predicting lots of changes that he did not have the energy to implement) officially told the world he was stepping down as Barcelona coach. The club announced that his successor would be his friend and assistant, Tito Vilanova – continuity guaranteed.

It was a year in which *La Liga* got away from Barça, who were stuck in second place from Matchday Nine onwards behind a remarkably efficient Real Madrid side that obtained a record 100 points. There remained one title to add, however: the twenty-sixth *Copa del Rey*, as Barcelona defeated Athletic Bilbao 3–0 at the Vicente Calderón in Madrid. Aside from the result, the match made the headlines because, just as had occurred in the clash between Catalans and Basques three years earlier in Valencia, both sets of supporters drowned out the Spanish National Anthem with boos, even though the abridged version had been played. Once again, football served as a vehicle for political protest.

Guardiola said goodbye to the supporters on May 5, during the last home game of the campaign against Espanyol. It was a night riddled with emotional moments. Messi scored all four goals, a giant banner was passed around the terraces saying: "We love you, Pep", and Guardiola addressed a few words to a packed-full stadium: "Thank you to every single one of you … because we have worked so hard day after day for you to be able to enjoy watching us play … See you soon, you will never lose me!" He ended up being thrown in the air by the players, while the crowd chanted his name.

2012–13: THE TITO VILANOVA YEAR

"It's an honour to be chosen as the man to continue this club's illustrious history," stated Tito Vilanova during his official unveiling in June 2012. Spain became European champions just two weeks later with five *Azulgranas* from La Masía in their starting eleven (Piqué, Busquets, Iniesta, Xavi and Fàbregas) and one on the bench (Pedro). One more, Jordi Alba, also a product of the Barça youth team, was signed just a few days after the tournament ended.

The *Supercopa* was contested in late August against Real Madrid, with a home triumph (3–2) and an away defeat (2–1) meaning *Los Merengues* came out victorious on away goals. The first half of the league campaign, however, was almost flawless: Barça picked up 55 from a possible 57 points, winning 18 and drawing just one game along the way. Messi was once again named the best player in the world on January 7 as the Argentinian star picked up his record-breaking fourth *Ballon d'Or*. He overtook legends such as Cruyff and Michel Platini, who had received three. Cristiano Ronaldo and Iniesta came second and third respectively.

The season was tainted, however, by the news that Vilanova's cancer of the parotid gland had returned, despite already having had surgery to remove it. He was forced to take temporary leave in December 2012 in order to have another operation. His assistant, Jordi Roura, took charge of the squad for a few weeks while Vilanova received chemotherapy and radiotherapy. He was back in the dugout on April 2 for the Champions League quarter-final against PSG. *La Liga* was all but sewn up, yet Real Madrid eliminated them in the *Copa del Rey* semi-final after a 1–1 draw at the Camp Nou and a 3–0 *Merengues* victory at the Bernabéu.

Barça made stuttering progress in the Champions League. After a 2–0 loss away to AC Milan in the last-16 first leg, they needed a spectacular home comeback, which arrived in the shape of a 4–0 victory, to continue fighting for the cup. Barça scraped past Paris Saint-Germain on away goals (2–2 and 1–1), but suffered a resounding defeat in the semi-final. That season's eventual winners, Bayern Munich, put four past the *Azulgranas* in the first leg and three past them in the second, before recruiting Guardiola for the subsequent season.

The league campaign reached its conclusion with the *Azulgranas* on a sensational 100 points, equalling the record set the previous year by Real Madrid, who ended on "only" 85. Barça also clinched the *Copa Catalunya*, although they needed a penalty shoot-out after a 1–1 draw with Espanyol. Those would be the two highlights of a season in which supporters had to resign themselves to losing fighter Eric Abidal, who announced his departure in May, having not renewed his contract. The Frenchman already knew that Víctor Valdés was leaving at the end of the 2014 campaign and that striker Villa had signed for Altético de Madrid.

The 2013–14 season began with a terribly painful hammer blow. Coach Tito Vilanova called sporting director Andoni Zubizarreta one Wednesday night in July to inform him that he was unable to continue as his cancer had returned. From that moment his fight was a different one. The club, that had provided endless support to the coach with whom they had commenced the campaign, had to find a new leader in one week. In the end president Sandro Rosell suggested to Zubizarreta the appointment of Gerardo "Tata" Martino, whom he had met during his tenure as Paraguay national coach.

The process was accelerated. The Argentine coach, who had just led Newell's Old Boys to championship glory, decided not to make wholesale changes to the squad. He opted to get to know them initially and the only big signing, sealed months earlier, was Brazilian international Neymar, who was considered a future candidate to win the *Ballon d'Or*. The team was deeply affected by the Bayern Munich defeat in the Champions League. Martino knew that he had to make some alterations in order for his side to continue competing and respecting the philosophy that had taken them so far.

The season began with a *Supercopa* victory against Atlético de Madrid, who would become Barça's main rival as the season progressed. In fact that title turned out to be the only one in a very complicated campaign. The Argentine coaching staff wanted to look for new ways to defeat teams that knew how to exploit Barcelona's weaknesses. However, the team's play suffered, yet individual talent was to thank for *Los Azulgranas* getting through various rounds in the Cup and Champions League, as well as spending 24 weeks on top of the pile in *La Liga*.

Martino's side put together a run of 20 matches unbeaten, reached the semi-finals of the Cup, comfortably defeated Manchester City in the Champions League last 16 and handed Rayo a 6–0 drubbing having lost the possession battle when the sides met earlier in the campaign. Everything seemed to be going according to plan, but a defeat by Real Sociedad in the New Year shattered the illusion as Xavi and Cesc Fàbregas looked on helplessly from the bench while Busquets and Song played in midfield.

There were also problems away from the pitch. President Sandro Rosell resigned following a lawsuit driven by Barcelona club member Jordi Cases that alleged he misappropriated funds from the signing of Neymar. "I don't want unfair attacks to affect the club's management and image negatively. That is why I think my time has come to an end," acknowledged Rosell. After his departure and once Neymar's father lifted the confidentiality pact over the operation, the club released detailed information regarding the cost of signing the Brazilian and figures relating to the player's salary as well as other agreements and previous investments.

Barcelona were defeated by Atlético de Madrid in the Champions League quarter finals and by the old enemy, Real Madrid, in the final of the *Copa*; and losses against lowly Valladolid and Granada meant their title challenge depended on slip-ups by Real Madrid and surprise package of the season Atlético, who became the opponent to beat for the two giants that had shared the previous nine titles between them.

The club looked to guarantee a healthy future with a referendum regarding the expansion and revamping of the Camp Nou and the surrounding areas, called the Nou Espai Barça, with a 600m euro investment. The supporters endorsed the project with more than 70 percent of the votes, but the club had to digest some bad news when FIFA announced a transfer ban until June 2015 for allegedly breaching rules on signing and registering minors. Barcelona felt victimized on various fronts and although they managed to get the sanction

suspended until January 2016, the warning sufficed to trigger a restructuring process across all levels of the clubs, no matter what happened that season.

Surprisingly, what happened that season was that Barcelona had the opportunity to win the league on the last day at the Camp Nou in a match between the top two teams, a situation which had not occurred since 1951. The *Azulgranas* simply had to beat Atlético, yet Martino did not select Xavi in the starting line-up, leaving him on the bench once again. The contest ended in a draw following yet another defensive error from a corner. Fans had arrived at the ground in droves to support a team in which they were fast losing faith. Once the final whistle confirmed Atlético's success, the home supporters gave the new champions a standing ovation and even chanted "Atleti, Atleti, Atleti!" which is usually only heard with such venom at the Calderón. It was an example of sportsmanship by fans who demanded changes.

The changes were not long in coming. Coach Martino said his goodbyes that very evening. Carles Puyol had already bidden farewell in a press conference, holding back the tears after 15 years and 21 titles with the first team. He left his mark with his exemplary behaviour which helped strengthen the club's real spirit during his

career. Another crucial player in Barcelona's most prolific period of glory, Victor Valdés, penned an open goodbye letter to the club. Two days later, Leo Messi put pen to paper on a new contract following a 41-goal tally despite two injury-hit months over a season in which nobody reached top form. He was to be the focal point of the new project headed by Luis Enrique, who was announced as the new Barcelona coach for the upcoming two campaigns on May 19, 2014.

The club was in need of a new direction. Big decisions were aimed at stabilizing it, including changes at La Masía and in the way the club was run. Another momentous blow would leave Barcelona in shock, however. Tito Vilanova – the coach who had begun the season, the assistant in the best year in Barcelona's history, the one with six titles, the coach who had won the league with a record 100 points, the *Azulgrana* with *"seny, pit i collons"* (Catalan for "common sense, strength and guts") – died on April 25, 2014, aged 45. By nature a man of the people, Vilanova left quite a legacy. His gentlemanly conduct and respect for both the opposition and those on his side mark the path that Barcelona plan to follow in order to remain at the illustrious heights which they have worked so hard to reach.

ABOVE: Former FC Barcelona midfielder and new coach Luis Enrique knows the club, the players, and even convinced legend Carles Puyol to the stay on and work with him. A fresh chapter in the Barcelona's history was about to begin.

ABOVE: Barça's season 2008–09 burst into life on September 21 with the *Azulgrana* putting six goals past Sporting de Gijón. The previous two league games had ended in defeat against Numancia and all-square against Racing de Santander. This is Barça's third goal.

LEFT: Messi, Xavi and Bojan Krkic celebrate another goal from the same match. The scorers were Eto'o, Xavi, Iniesta, Messi (two) and an own goal by Sporting's Jorge. Maldonado scored a consolation goal for the home side.

RIGHT and BELOW: Moments from the 2–6 victory at the Bernabéu on May 2, 2009. On the right, one of Thierry Henry's goals. Below, the players celebrate the momentous result at the final whistle. It signalled the start of a period of dominant *Azulgrana* victories over the old enemy. The dejected figure of Real Madrid goalkeeper Iker Casillas can be seen in the foreground.

"We are almost like disciples of the principle that Cruyff founded here."
Pep Guardiola

BELOW: Andrés Iniesta celebrates his stunning goal against Chelsea in the 93rd minute of the second leg of the Champions League semi-final at Stamford Bridge, which took Barcelona to the final in Rome on May 27, 2009 against Manchester United.

TOP RIGHT: The 2009 Champions League final proved to be a triumphant night for Barça. Samuel Eto'o opened the scoring and Lionel Messi scored Barça's second with a perfectly placed looping header. Manchester United's Rio Ferdinand and Edwin van der Sar can only watch as the decisive blow is delivered.

BELOW LEFT: Lionel Messi and Andrés Iniesta lift the prestigious trophy following Barça's 2–0 victory in the Champions League final over Manchester United. It was the club's third trophy of the 2008-09 campaign, after clinching the league title and the *Copa del Rey*.

BELOW RIGHT: Coach Pep Guardiola is tossed in the air by his players at the close of the match that won Barcelona's third European Cup, after Wembley in 1992 and Paris in 2006. Before the year came to an end, Barcelona would also lift the *Supercopa*, the European Super Cup and the Club World Cup – six titles in one glorious year.

FOLLOWING PAGES: The 2–1 victory over Estudiantes de la Plata in Abu Dhabi in the FIFA Club World Cup was a fitting end to a marvellous year. The Argentine side had taken the lead in the first half through Mauro Boselli, but Pedro equalized with one minute remaining in normal time. Lionel Messi scored the winning goal five minutes into the second half of extra time.

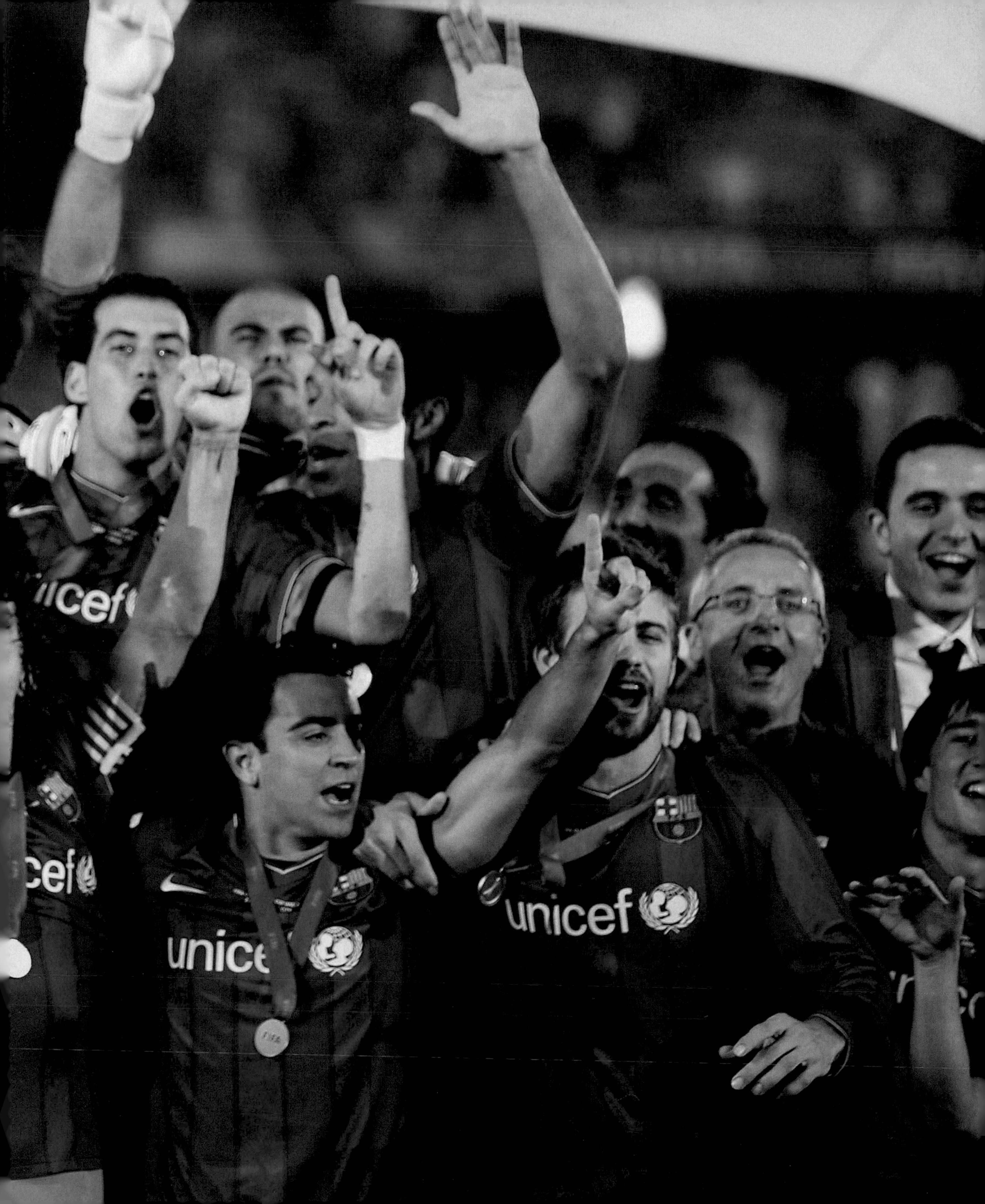
unicef
unicef
unicef

"In the football world there is only one secret: either I have the ball or I don't have it."
Pep Guardiola

ABOVE: The world listens to the Spanish National Anthem before the World Cup Final against the Netherlands in Johannesburg. The players in this photo (Xavi, Pedro, Carles Puyol, Gerard Piqué, Sergio Busquets and Iniesta) formed the backbone of Guardiola's Barcelona team. The *Azulgrana* style of play would hugely influence *La Roja* during the triumphant tournament.

RIGHT: Former team-mates Carles Puyol and Ronaldinho meet in August 2010 during the Joan Gamper Trophy. FC Barcelona won the game on penalties following a 1–1 stalemate with AC Milan. The match was a tribute to "the Gaucho" who was given the 45th Joan Gamper Trophy as a gift by his former team-mates. New signings David Villa, Javier Mascherano and Adriano all featured.

"I could forgive any mistake, but I will not forgive anyone who doesn't give his heart and soul to Barcelona."
Pep Guardiola

BELOW: Lionel Messi celebrates the first of two goals against Real Madrid at the Bernabéu in the Champions League semi-final first leg on April 27, 2011. The 1–1 draw in the second leg was not enough for *Los Blancos*, who had to watch on as the old enemy progressed to the much-anticipated Wembley final.

ABOVE: The 2011 Champions League final against Manchester United was a repeat of the 2009 final in Rome. Barça's Pedro opened the scoring after 27 minutes and second-half goals from Lionel Messi and David Villa secured an emphatic 3–1 win.

RIGHT: One of the most moving moments of the 2011 Champions League final came when Eric Abidal, who had just fought off liver cancer, was given the trophy by captain Carles Puyol to lift in front of the supporters.

FOLLOWING PAGES: The entire FC Barcelona squad celebrates *Copa del Rey* success after beating Athletic Bilbao 3–0 at the Vicente Calderón on May 25, 2012. Barça have won more *Copas del Rey* than any other side (26), this one being the most recent. The Barça goalscorers were Pedro (two) and Lionel Messi.

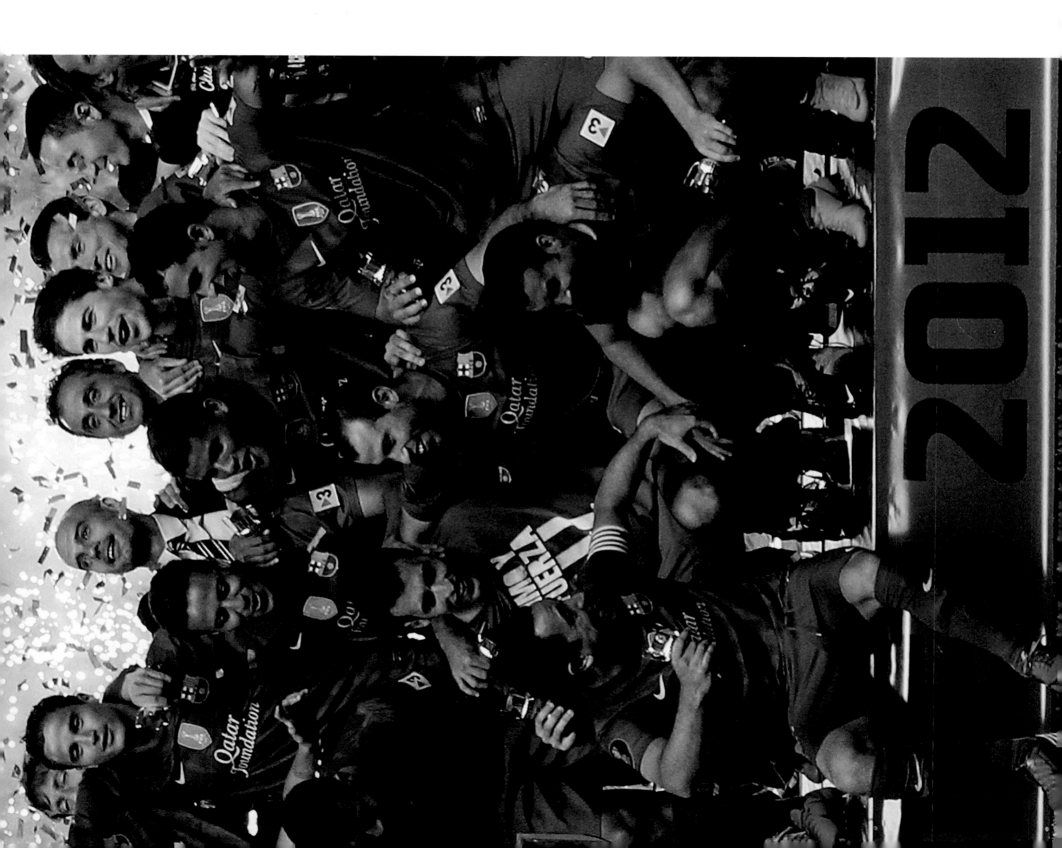

ABOVE: Pep Guardiola's final match in charge at the Camp Nou was against RCD Espanyol on May 5, 2012. Supporters filled the ground to wish him an emotional farewell. A giant banner saying, "We love you, Pep" summed up the feelings of the *culé* supporters, who chanted his name incessantly. Guardiola closed his speech by saying: "I'll see you soon, you'll never lose me!"

ABOVE RIGHT: FC Barcelona pulled off an epic comeback against AC Milan in the second leg of the European Cup last 16 tie on March 12, 2013. After a disappointing 2–0 defeat in Milan, a Messi brace (in minutes 5 and 40) followed by goals from Villa (52) and Jordi Alba (92) smoothed Barça's passage to the quarter-finals. The photograph shows David Villa scoring the third.

BELOW RIGHT: Jordi Alba and Dani Alves celebrate the fourth goal and their place in the next round. Assistant coach Jordi Roura was in the dugout in Vilanova's absence.

ABOVE: Barça's only silverware of the season, *La Liga*, arrived in style, the *Azulgranas* sitting at the top of the pile during the entire campaign and equalling Real Madrid's record points tally (100) from the season before. Tito Vilanova and Eric Abidal lift the trophy after the Valladolid match on May 19, 2013, at the Camp Nou.

RIGHT: The victory parade through the whole of Barcelona took place a few days earlier on May 13, 2013, to celebrate Barcelona's league triumph after 35 games, which was secured when Real Madrid drew 1–1 with RCD Espanyol.

ABOVE LEFT: Club president Sandro Rosell managed to sign the new star in the football constellation in 2013. Two of the world's best players, Neymar and Messi, continuing to play together makes for a fascinating prospect in the seasons to come.

LEFT: The 2013–14 season was difficult for Barca. With a new coach arriving from another football culture (the Argentine Tata Martino) and with a group that had won a lot and needed new blood, FC Barcelona ended up with only one minor title that season, the Spanish *Supercopa*.

ABOVE RIGHT: A defeat in the 2013–14 Champions League against Ajax, the historical inspiration of the club, did some damage even if it didn't prevent them from qualifying for the competition's group stages. The result prompted doubts about the manager. Tata Martino would only be at the club for one season.

RIGHT: But Barcelona has got some very talented players, who were able to raise their level in certain moments of the season. Leo Messi enjoyed scoring against Real Madrid at the Santiago Bernabéu. The victory benefited Atlético de Madrid, the surprising 2013–14 *La Liga* winners.

SAMUEL ETO'O

Born in Nkon, Cameroon, in 1981, Samuel Eto'o was one of the most important and influential players in Barcelona's recent history. Cameroon's captain and top scorer was a striker who never gave up and possessed an insatiable hunger for goals. The "Indomitable Lion" had an explosive personality and a frightening burst of pace.

He was playing for Mallorca when Barça signed him in 2004, after an arduous battle with Real Madrid, who owned half his transfer rights. By that time he had already been named the African Player of the Year in 2003 (which he won again in 2004 and 2005, and later in 2010 as an Inter player). It was a wise move to sign him, clearly shown by his 108 league goals in five seasons as an *Azulgrana*, to which he added another 22 in all other competitions. The statistics show that he is one of the best strikers ever to have played for the club. Under both Rijkaard and Guardiola, his decisive goals and hunger for victory in certain matches was crucial for sealing some of Barça's most important titles.

His exemplary behaviour on the pitch was in contrast to his fiery character, which brought him a fair few problems. During Rijkaard's last season in the dugout, he made some statements lambasting Sandro Rosell, Ronaldinho and the coach himself. Maybe that is why Guardiola initially thought about letting him go when he took over as coach. He revealed as much in a press conference, but the combination of an impressive pre-season and his change in attitude triggered by Deco and Ronaldinho leaving the club made Guardiola revoke his decision, and Eto'o stayed at Barça for one more season.

During his final season as an *Azulgrana*, Eto'o became one of the most crucial members of the team, even when he had to play on the right wing to leave space for Messi down the middle. Alongside the Argentinian and Thierry Henry, he formed part of a devastating attacking trio that netted 100 goals between them. It was Eto'o who opened the scoring in both the Paris and Rome Champions League finals.

In spite of his sterling performances, Guardiola decided to do without him for the following season, when he moved to Inter in exchange for the Swede Zlatan Ibrahimović. That move meant he went on to be the only player in history to win a treble (in this case, the Champions League, league and domestic cup) in successive seasons, in 2009 with FC Barcelona and in 2010 with Inter.

"The team can function without me, as no one player is untouchable. Barça have players of the highest quality."
Samuel Eto'o

XAVI HERNÁNDEZ

Born in Terrassa, Catalonia, in 1980, Xavi joined FC Barcelona in 1991 at the age of just 11. He attended La Masía, and Barça was the club where he grew up, debuted, matured and became one of the world's best central midfielders.

After some years in the B team, he made a goalscoring first-team debut on August 18, 1998, under Van Gaal in the *Supercopa* against Mallorca. He appeared in a further 16 games that season and consolidated his position the following year, when an injury to his idol Guardiola saw him promoted to first-team regular, a position which he would make his own once his predecessor left for Brescia. He is a playmaker with superb vision, the ability to play quick, short passes, excellent anticipation and a knack for keeping possession.

He has worn the *Azulgrana* colours more than any other player, having overtaken Migueli in 2010. His 14 seasons in the first team have provided him with more titles than anyone else, 21 at the time of writing: seven *La Ligas*, two *Copas del Rey*, five *Supercopas*, two European Super Cups, two World Club Cups and three Champions Leagues.

As an international, he was the leader of the side that won the 1999 FIFA U-20 World Cup and a silver medal at the Olympic Games in Sydney. His full international debut arrived on November 15, 2000, and his presence has been a key element in the team ever since. The *La Roja* shirt, which he has worn more than 100 times, has seen him win Euro 2008 against Germany (he assisted Fernando Torres for the winning goal), and he was chosen by UEFA as the player of the championship. He was crowned world champion in South Africa in 2010 and was chosen for the team of the tournament. A 4–0 victory over Italy saw him become a Euro 2012 winner, too. Without being a regular goalscorer, he still managed to score Spain's one-thousandth goal.

As well as team titles, Xavi has an impressive collection of individual accolades, with 1999 *La Liga* Breakthrough Player of the Year and Spanish Player of the Year in 2005 two of the standouts. Other successes include the International Federation of Football History and Statistics (IFFHS) World's Best Playmaker award in 2008, 2009, 2010 and 2011; a hat trick of third-place finishes in the *Ballon d'Or* in 2009, 2010 and 2011; runner-up in the 2011 UEFA Best Player in Europe Award and FIFA Club World Cup Silver Ball winner, also in 2011; and the Prince of Asturias Award for Sports (shared with Iker Casillas) in 2012.

His leadership in the national team, alongside Real Madrid's Casillas, made it easier to overcome the tension between the clubs during the overdose of *clásicos* in the Mourinho era.

"Thinking quickly is more important than moving quickly."
Xavi Hernández

LIONEL MESSI

It is a difficult task to sum up the CV of the man considered by most fans, experts, players and journalists to be the best player in the world and, maybe, of all time. Messi was born in Rosario, Argentina, in 1987 and arrived at the age of 13 at FC Barcelona from the youth ranks of Newell's Old Boys, once the Catalan club had agreed to pay for Messi's growth hormone deficiency treatment.

Along with Fàbregas and Piqué, he rapidly rose up through the various categories after immediately showing that he was much more than an average talent. His first-team debut, when he was still a youngster, came in a friendly against Porto on November 16, 2003, under Frank Rijkaard. In the 2004–05 season, he flittered between Barcelona B and the first team, with the Dutchman selecting him nine times in all competitions.

At 17 years old, he became the *Azulgranas'* youngest-ever player with his first goal arriving in a league match against Albacete, from a Ronaldinho pass. He was a regular starter in the 2005–06 season, in which Barça won *La Liga* and their second Champions League against Arsenal, a campaign in which he actively participated, although he missed the final in Paris through injury. By the next season, the Number 19 was already one of the first names on the team sheet, as he was the team's second-best goalscorer behind Ronaldinho. A memorable strike against Getafe in the *Copa del Rey* has gone down in history for being almost identical to Maradona's goal against England in the 1986 World Cup. He also netted a hat trick in a 3–3 draw against Real Madrid that season.

managed to net 38 goals during the treble season, including a header in the Champions League final against Manchester United and a brace in the 2–6 win at the Bernabéu.

Even more convincing evidence arrived the following season in the shape of 47 goals, composed of a four-goal flurry against Arsenal in the Champions League, three hat tricks and ten braces. Guardiola said in a press conference that he was the "best player I have ever seen" and made him the focal point of the team. This gave Messi space to perform, and the coach also made the other forwards in the squad adapt so that the Argentinian could develop as a footballer.

Since then, his relentless growth has continued, allowing him to break almost all possible records, such as being the only footballer with four *Ballons d'Or* to his name. His hat trick against Osasuna in 2013–14 took him past Paulino Alcántara's goalscoring record of 371 goals (344 in official matches and 27 in friendlies). Just one week later, the Argentinian netted another three goals, including the winner in a memorable 3–4 victory at the Bernabéu.

As for the Argentina national team, he won the FIFA World Youth Championship and a gold medal at the Beijing Olympics in 2008. He is currently his country's captain, having been handed the skipper's armband by Alejandro Sabella in 2011.

"It has been an honour to be the coach of the best

CLUB HONOURS

EUROPEAN CUP/
UEFA CHAMPIONS LEAGUE: 4
(1991–92, 2005–06, 2008–09, 2010–11)

FIFA CLUB WORLD CUP: 2
(2009–10, 2011–12)

EUROPEAN CUP WINNERS' CUP/
UEFA CUP WINNERS' CUP: 4
(1978–79, 1981–82, 1988–89, 1996–97)

INTER–CITIES FAIRS CUP: 3
(1957–58, 1959–60, 1965–66
(Barcelona won the trophy outright in a
special tournament held in1971)

EUROPEAN SUPER CUP: 4
(1992–93, 1997–98, 2009–10, 2011–12)

LATIN CUP: 2
(1948–49, 1951–52)

COPA DE LOS PIRINEOS: 4
(1909–10, 1910–11, 1911–12, 1912–13)
Unofficial Competition

LIGA: 22
1928–29, 1944–45, 1947–48, 1948–49, 1951–52,
1952–53, 1958–59, 1959–60, 1973–74, 1984–85,
1990–91, 1991–92, 1992–93, 1993–94, 1997–98,
1998–99, 2004–05, 2005–06, 2008–09, 2009–10,
2010–11, 2012–2013

COPA DEL REY: 26
1909–10, 1911–12, 1912–13, 1919–20, 1921–22,
1924–25, 1925–26, 1927–28, 1941–42, 1950–51,
1951–52, 1952–53, 1956–57, 1958–59, 1962–63,
1967–68, 1970–71, 1977–78, 1980–81, 1982–83,
1987–88, 1989–90, 1996–97, 1997–98, 2008–09,
2011–12

LEFT: It is about winning. But also how you win. Those that have followed Barcelona have fallen in love with Leo Messi, his team-mates and with what they represented.

SUPERCOPA DE ESPAÑA: 11
(1983–84, 1991–92, 1992–93, 1994–95, 1996–97,
2005–06, 2006–07, 2009–10, 2010–11, 2011–12,
2013–14)
• **COPA DE LA LIGA:** 2
(1982–83, 1985–86)
• **LIGA MEDITERRÁNEA:** 1
(1937)
• **LIGA CATALANA:** 1
(1937–38)
• **CAMPEONATO DE CATALUNYA:** 23
1901–02, 1902–03, 1904–05, 1908–09, 1909–10,
1910–11, 1912–13, 1915–16, 1918–19, 1919–20,
1920–21, 1921–22, 1923–24, 1924–25, 1925–26,
1926–27, 1927–28, 1929–30, 1930–31, 1931–32,
1934–35, 1935–36, 1937–38 (including its
precursors Copa Macaya (1901–02) and Copa
Barcelona (1902–03))

COPA CATALUNYA: 7
(1990–91, 1992–93, 1999–2000, 2003–04,
2004–05, 2006–07, 2012–13) (until 1993–94, Copa
Generalitat)

COPA EVA DUARTE: 2
(1948, 1952)

Spain's Primera División was inaugurated in
the 1928–29 season and FC Barcelona were
the first team proclaimed champions. Until that
time, Spanish football was organized around
the Campeonato de España. The first champions
and sub–champions of the *Campeonato de España*
competed in its first few seasons. From 1934–35,
the number of teams was increased, going up to 12.

Until today, Barça have won 22 Spanish league
titles, second to Real Madrid's 32, and clear of
third placed Atlético de Madrid with 9 and Athletic
Bilbao with 8.

INDEX

CREDITS

The publishers would like to thank the following sources for their kind permission to reproduce the pictures in this book:

AKG IMAGES: /Mel Longhurst: 16R

FC BARCELONA: 10–11, 13, 14T, 16L, 17, 18, 19, 20, 20–21, 21, 22, 23, 26–27, 28, 29, 32, 33L, 33R, 36T, 36B, 37, 38T, 39T; /Atelier Helios: 12, 25; /Jordi Clemente: 14B; *Los Deportes*: 15; /Ramon Dimas: 35, 38B, 39B; /Miguel Morata Royes: 40T; /Miguel Ruiz: 140–141; /J. A. Saenz Guerrero: 41; /Josep Segrelles: 30; /Horacio Segui: 44–45, 46, 50, 51, 57L, 58, 62L, 62R, 63T, 63C, 63B, 64, 65T, 65B, 66, 68R, 79, 83, 87, 90TL, 90TR, 90B, 91T, 91B, 92–93, 98–99, 101, 105, 107, 109, 132; /TAF: 40B

FC Barcelona has made every effort to contact the copyright holders of all photographs. Any liability for these images being reproduced is the responsibility of the publishers.

GETTY IMAGES: /Ahmad Al-Rubaye/AFP: 168–169; /Allsport: 89; /Gonzalo Arroyo Moreno: 177B; /John Berry: 181T; /Bongarts: 129; /Shaun Botterill: 136, 143, 173T; /Clive Brunskill: 80; /Eric Cabanis/AFP: 134; /David Cannon: 94B; /Sigfrid Casals/Cover: 73; /Phil Cole: 133; /Carl de Souza/AFP: 173B; /Denis Doyle: 112, 171; /Gianni Ferrari/Cover: 55; /Ruediger Fessel/Bongarts: 127; /Stu Forster: 120, 128B; /Lluis Gene/AFP: 4–5, 110–111, 124, 158–159, 166, 176, 177T,

179; /Laurence Griffiths: 167BL, 188; /Alexander Hassenstein: 145, 152; /Mike Hewitt: 160; /Jasper Juinen: 125, 148-149, 183; /Josep Lago/AFP: 8-9, 150, 156; /Alex Livesey: 172; /Angel Martinez: 174–175; /Clive Mason: 130–131; /Pascal Pavani/AFP: 123; /Popperfoto: 126, 127; /Dani Pozo/AFP: 181B; /Gary M Prior: 102–103; /Manuel Queimadelos Alonso: 187; /Ben Radford: 114; /David Ramos: 6, 178, 180T, 180B, 185; /Cesar Rangel/AFP: 116–117, 147; /Miguel Riopa/AFP: 164T, 164B; /Miguel Ruiz: 163; /STR/AFP: 165B; /Roberto Schmidt/AFP: 170; /Christophe Simon/AFP: 135, 137; /Javier Soriano/AFP: 154, 165T; /Bob Thomas: 57R, 67, 68L, 69, 71, 74–75, 76, 84, 88-89, 94T, 95, 100, 138, 139, 167T, 167BR; /VI Images: 52, 96, 97, 119

OFFSIDE SPORTS PHOTOGRAHY: /L'Equipe: 43, 61; /Marca: 48

PRESS ASSOCIATION IMAGES: /Topham Picturepoint: 60

Every effort has been made to acknowledge correctly and contact the source and/or copyright holder of each picture, and Carlton Books Limited apologizes for any unintentional errors or omissions that will be corrected in future editions of this book.

Special thanks to Marcel Russiñol Amat at the Research and Documentation Centre of FC Barcelona, for all of his hard work and expertise on this project.